David H.J. Delcorde

450232

P9-CRR-024

The *Art* of BUSINESS AND MANAGEMENT

CASE ANALYSIS

Kendall Hunt
publishing company

Cover image © Shutterstock.com

Kendall Hunt
publishing company

www.kendallhunt.com
Send all inquiries to:
4050 Westmark Drive
Dubuque, IA 52004-1840

Copyright © 2019 by Kendall Hunt Publishing Company

ISBN: 978-1-7924-0232-6

All rights reserved. No part of this publication may be reproduced,
stored in a retrieval system, or transmitted, in any form or by any means,
electronic, mechanical, photocopying, recording, or otherwise,
without the prior written permission of the copyright owner.

Published in the United States of America

For Cindi....

This one's for you

Contents

Contents

MARKETING CASES

About the Author

Dr. David H. J. Delcorde is the Director of Undergraduate Programs at the Telfer School of Management, University of Ottawa, Ottawa, Canada, where he has taught courses in business and management since 2002. He has also enjoyed a rewarding career in the Canadian federal public service spanning over thirty years, retiring as a member of the executive cadre. And is now a farmer ☺

Dr. Delcorde completed his undergraduate degree in business administration at the University of Ottawa; a Master of Business Administration (MBA) degree from Heriot-Watt University, Edinburgh, Scotland; a Master of Arts in International Business Management from the University of Westminster in London, England, and a Doctorate in Philosophy from London South Bank University in London, England.

Dr. Delcorde is the author of the textbook, "Canadian Business and Society," also published by Kendall Hunt.

N.B. *All persons and companies appearing in this book are fictitious. Any resemblance to actual persons or real companies is purely coincidental.*

Preface

An understanding of business case analysis is essential for the student of business and management. This book is intended for the neophyte business student and will demonstrate how business concepts are applied.

Introduction

While there are other ways to finesse the determinants of an organization's success, the success of most organizations depends on the effective interaction of three key constituents: people, stakeholders, and money. *People* include an organization's human resources, frequently the sole source of competitive advantage, the effective and efficient management of which requires an understanding of organizational behaviour and culture at both the "national culture" level as well as the "organizational culture level." *Stakeholders* include those individuals, groups, and organizations with an actual or perceived stake or interest in the organization's activities and the ability to exert direct or indirect influence on those activities. The broad range of stakeholders typically includes an organization's owners, employees, suppliers, and competitors, and can frequently include government and civil society organizations. Given the importance of effective cash flow management to all organizations, as well as an understanding of the importance of record-keeping, financial risk management (the risk-return trade-off), *money* in this context refers to a basic understanding of accounting, finance, and *cash flow* principles.

Entrenched in all three constituents is ethics, social responsibility, and globalization, which collectively complicate the work needed for continuing success. The treatment of *ethics* is more complicated than simply "acting ethically." Taking the obviously right course of action when compared to taking the obviously wrong course of action is not a particularly difficult decision to make. The challenge occurs when a decision must be made to take a course of action from among two or more obviously right courses of action: a possible definition of an ethical dilemma. Whatever the decision, the results will affect people, a range of stakeholders, and money.

Social responsibility concerns the extent to which the organization should act in such a way as to consciously and deliberately consider how its activities affect society and assume responsibility for its actions. The use of *"the extent to which..."* above is intentional. While it is essential that organizations act in a socially responsible manner, socially responsible activities are not free. Some of the questions become: What is the correct amount of "social responsibility"? Do all key stakeholders concur with the amount of social responsibility undertaken? If the organization meets the minimum expectations of society, is the organization socially responsible or simply not socially *irresponsible*? Who in society decides what is acceptable (which stakeholders)?

Globalization can be viewed as the convergence of markets, organizations, and ideas into an inter-related, interdependent, and often symbiotic business, government, and civil society international landscape. Globalization as a concept has its own group of stakeholders—those who support and those who denounce its claimed virtues.

Ultimately, organizations find themselves in the midst of this complicated landscape. While a working knowledge of the core disciplines in business, government, and civil society are important, the ability to strategically understand their application, interaction, and integration is critical for success.

While the focus of this book is essentially business, the use of "organizations" in preceding paragraphs is intentional—case analysis is not restricted to business but is found in many areas: health, education, government, analytics, and social sciences to mention just a few.

The use of case studies represents a form of active learning in which realistic scenarios are presented to learners who are required to apply their knowledge and reason in arriving at a position, recommendation,

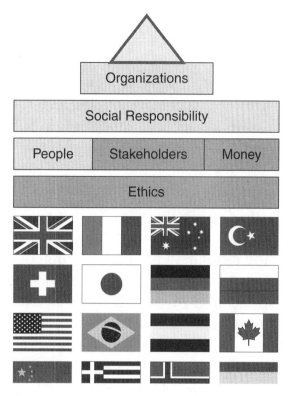

Figure I The Environment of Organizations

Source: © Aleksa2013/Shutterstock.com

Adapted by Kendall Hunt Publishing Company

or a course of action. There are rarely absolutely "right" and absolutely "wrong" responses to case analysis, but rather responses that are stronger than others based upon the extent to which the respondent has taken all aspects of the case study into account. This raises a number of questions: (1) What approaches to case analysis might be available? (2) Are there approaches that are better suited for cases that are grounded in, say, finance or human resources management? (3) What aspects of a case should be taken into account? (4) How long should a case analysis be? These and other questions will be considered in subsequent sections.

The purpose of this book is to provide some guidance for students in tackling a case study. Notwithstanding the macro environment in which organizations must operate, case studies differ in their complexity and requirements. For example, some case studies are presented more as "vignettes" that require responses to specific questions. Other case studies are long and complicated with somewhat "less-directed" requirements. While this book will explore both styles of cases, it is not intended to be perceived as the only, or the best approaches as many scholars would have different viewpoints. The book is intended to help students understand the importance of case analysis in the application of their contextual knowledge, and to suggest approaches to cases that will catalyze their ability to think confidently in developing a strong and reasoned response anchored in the foundations that are embedded in every case study. A further section of this book will consider the application of case studies to examinations.

No book is the product of one individual. Over the years, I have had the privilege of learning from, and working with, some of the best minds and intellectual thinkers, both academics and practitioners, in whose presence I am humbled—I am grateful for the lessons and the journey; and the journey continues...

Case Analysis: "Generalized Observations"

Many students are immediately concerned when faced with completing a case analysis. In comparison to the predominant approach to assignments that generally features a "binary" pedagogical approach (*for example, what are the main functions of the manager and provide an example of each…*), a case study represents unknown territory that falls outside a student's usual comfort zone (a prerequisite to catalyze thinking and learning that goes beyond simple memorization and "recall by rote"). There are many reasons for this:

1. The case study presents a "story" or a "scenario" that contains a large quantity of information; by its nature, with some redundancy, but for the most part important and often subtle;

2. Frequently there is no clear starting point or magical rubric that provides guidance on how to approach arriving at the optimal outcome;

3. Case studies vary in the initial perception of their focus;

4. A case study that appears to be "short" can in practice be significantly more complicated than its multipage counterpart;

5. Case studies typically touch a full spectrum of issues, with varying degrees of importance when considered individually, however when each issue is considered in terms of whether it has an impact on other issues, the case can greatly increase in complexity;

6. Case studies may have specific requirements in terms of requiring responses to specific questions, or the case study requirements may be of a more "open" nature: *What recommendations can you give to the Chief Executive Officer (CEO)*; while the latter style would be more challenging for obvious reasons, the requirements of a fully developed response to specific questions require considerable rigor;

7. Case analyses are often assigned to random groups of students, many of whom do not know each other; and there are the typical inherent challenges of group work serving to complicate an already complicated assignment! To deal with this idea of "groups and teams" a subsequent section of this book has been added below.

When these generalizations are considered together, a case analysis can be a fair representation of the "real" world in which students will ultimately find themselves. Whether a student's area of specialization is in a business-related field or any other area of specialization, it is necessary to consider the organization as a whole, and any issue being analyzed, from the perspective of the organization. For example, in the business context, a course of action that makes perfect sense from a marketing perspective may have little traction from a finance perspective. Similarly a course of action that would result in gaining market share may not be viable without the necessary human resource complement to put the action in place; *you need to have the horses to pull the load* as they say back on the farm!

Common Case Errors

After having graded a multitude of case studies from students ranging from first year college through graduate level university, I have found several common errors. Being aware of the common errors will help students avoid them!

1. Failing to understand precisely what is "required" and the context of the role the student is being asked to assume. For example: *"You are a consultant hired by the Beeming Company. Prepare a report that summarizes your recommendations on a course of action that would result in greater market share in East Asia."* Among other things, in this scenario you are a paid consultant, not an employee. The focus of your recommendations will be on market share in East Asia—not, for example, increasing market share globally;

2. Not reading the case with sufficient precision in order to differentiate the relevant from the irrelevant;

3. Not understanding the key issue and the supplementary issues that underline it. For example, consider the following greatly simplified fictitious scenario: *A company is experiencing decreasing domestic sales of its product and, in exploring exporting as means to generate revenue, has identified a foreign country in which there would be significant demand for this product, but has been unsuccessful in its efforts to sell this product in the specified foreign country.* Is the key issue "decreasing domestic sales" or the "inability to sell its product in the foreign country"? If the latter, is the supplementary issue non-tariff barriers imposed by the specified foreign country (import quotas, local content requirement), or tariffs, or something else?

4. Making incorrect, unrelated, illogical, oversimplifying or overcomplicating assumptions. This loaded statement requires further discussion. An assumption is something that might be reasonably accepted without any substantiation. Any assumptions made in case studies should pass three important tests: (1) is the assumption "reasonable," given the information at hand; (2) would a

casual reader concur with the assumption, and (3) would an informed reader concur with the assumption? *For example, in reviewing a set of financial statements representing the financial position and condition of a sole proprietorship, would the assumption that these statements were prepared on an accrual basis be reasonable?* A casual reader who lacks a basic understanding of financial accounting would possibly see no relevance to the assumption, or in other words, agree with the assumption. On the other hand, a Certified Public Accountant would consider the same assumption with a much different lens. Any assumption must logically be grounded in the material at hand and must not be made with a view to oversimplify a case. In other words, despite the definition of an assumption, there must be some compelling basis to making it—if the assumption is made to deliberately simplify a scenario; the writer is being manipulative, not analytical. At the same time, assumptions can make a case study more complicated than it actually is.

In the previous example regarding the review of financial statements, suppose there was an interest in the amount of depreciation expensed. *Depreciation* is the gradual diminishing value of a capital asset over time due to use, the expense component being allocated systematically over the useful life of the asset to ensure consistency with the "matching principle." Unlike a travel expense that reflects the actual costs of a trip for which cash was disbursed in the same amount to cover the costs, depreciation is an expense that does not involve the disbursement of cash in the same amount as the depreciation expense claimed. So what is the impact on statements prepared on a cash basis versus an accrual basis?

5. Arriving at a recommendation that is not supported by the analysis. For example, recommending global expansion of a company through a *greenfield* approach when the risk factors include an

unstable government, an unfavourable political ideology, and policy instruments—the combination of these factors would suggest excessive risk and therefore argue for *simple exporting* as a lower-risk option.

6. Misinterpreting quantitative data and/or overemphasizing quantitative data while underemphasizing qualitative data and/or failing to use an appropriate balance of both data types in developing a reasoned response.

7. Overusing graphics: A picture might be worth a thousand words, as the saying goes, but it is not a substitute for a well-written, thoughtful explanation.

8. Writing too much (cases are not graded by weight) or writing too little (attempts at precision must capture the full measure of the case).

9. Overemphasizing a particular part of the case study.

These common errors can be easily overcome by exercising judgement and rigour in the development of the final case analysis.

Before exploring some approaches to case analysis, it is strongly recommended that readers consider the next section on how to work effectively in a group.

Working in a Group or Team—Toward Effective Results on Case Analyses

To be theoretically correct (but recognizing some colleagues may not share my thesis on this one) the first encounter of members would constitute a *group* meeting and this would evolve into a *team* as the group dynamic matures. The discussion that follows will use the nomenclature team.

Your first encounter with team members to tackle your first case study involves sitting with fellow students you may not know and working on an assignment that is complicated, regardless of how benign the exercise initially appears. The following practices have assisted students in developing strong and reasoned responses to case studies working in a team paradigm.

1. Take the time to get to know your colleagues: What are their interests? What are they studying (their areas of specialization)? What do they enjoy?

2. If you are experiencing structural problems in your team, bring these to the attention of your instructor as soon as possible.

3. Have every team member read the case study thoroughly and identify those areas of the case study in which they have interest and/or expertise and/or talent. For example, a team member may be an accounting major; another team member may enjoy researching academic journals or popular press articles; another team member may be skilled at presentations (if the case so requires). Then match the available talent to the requirements.

4. Be certain to understand the requirements—if this is not clear, ask your professor or teaching assistant.

5. Be certain to schedule regular meetings (a combination of face-to-face and online is recommended) to measure progress and review work. Case studies are generally major pieces of work—do not leave this to the last possible minute.

6. As this is a <u>team</u> project, the grade earned by the team will apply to every member of the team; do not take a proprietary approach

to your section of the work—share your work and the work of others and do so frequently.

7. Have a team member be responsible for overall quality control— verifying references and citations, spelling and grammar, and generally ensuring that all requirements of the case assignment have been met.

8. Have someone who is not a student, read your response to ensure clarity of messaging.

9. Once the graded assignment is returned, take the necessary time to review the comments provided by the corrector—above all, this is a learning experience and the feedback obtained will be important moving forward when working on subsequent cases.

10. The best pedagogical approaches will typically require some form of "peer feedback" in which team members provide feedback on the performance of other team members. Note that the exercise of providing feedback is intended to be positive and constructive with a view to suggesting areas in which your colleagues could improve the effectiveness of their participation.

Approaches to Case Analysis

At the outset, it should be recognized that in my view, there is no "one size fits all" approach to developing responses to case analysis: The range of subject matter and the complexity of the requirements would make a single, universal approach untenable. There are, however, two key styles of cases as mentioned earlier: (1) cases that require responses to specific questions and (2) cases that require a response that is more "open ended." This book will explore both styles and provide some "solved" examples. Furthermore, a "guiding rubric" will be provided that will delineate features and characteristics of the response(s) that fail to meet expectations compared with those that "meet" and "exceed" expectations. These rubrics are intended to serve as guidance only—individual instructors may have different requirements.

Regardless of case style, the following initial steps are recommended:

1. Read the case thoroughly before considering the actual requirements;

2. Read the requirements;

3. Read the case again, with the requirements in mind, and highlight what you feel are the relevant components;

4. Compare what you have highlighted with the requirements; and

5. Think about how you would approach responding to the case requirements.

Style 1—Cases that Require Responses to Specific Questions

The first style of case to be considered is one in which specific questions are asked. The response will depend on the questions. Consider the following example:

Leadership in Human Resources Operations at DRP

The Department of Rare Plants (DRP) is a large, complex federal government department. Many employees are scientists while others are naturalists, and paramilitary types whose job is to ensure the safety and security of naturally occurring rare plants across the country. The mandate of DRP also extends to plants found in ocean beds and shoals occurring to the full extent of the 200 mile exclusive economic zone as well as freshwater lake beds (including the Great Lakes). Many of the employees at DRP have worked in the department for years. The culture is a supportive one with employees genuinely caring about one another and most managers are supportive.

The Human Resources Directorate consists of twenty-five employees headed by Benjamin McGraw who served, until recently, as the Director of this unit for over eight years. Benjamin was sixty years old and had spent his entire career in Human Resources, starting as a staffing officer "back in the day" when it was called "Personnel."

This directorate is very operational. It is concerned with staffing, compensation, training, and labour relations and providing these services to 7,000 employees. The nature of this work generally involves applying a plethora of policies and guidelines to human resources requests made by operational managers. As such there is always a need to interpret policies made by Central Agencies and apply this interpretation to the actions being proposed by operational managers.

Of the twenty-five staff, most are employees at junior levels of the personnel administration classification group—PE-02 or PE-03. McGraw himself is a PE-06 (the most senior level in this category). The employees typically are young and have varying degrees of expertise and experience, despite being at the same classification level. This is partly to do with practice of promoting employees quickly in order to reduce turnover (if you don't promote them, some other department will), as PE employees are in shortage in the federal government, and partly due to varying practices and expectations in different departments. For example, in small departments and agencies, a PE-02 or PE-03 might be expected to provide a broader range of services, becoming more of a generalist than a specialist. For the employees of the Human Resources Directorate, the days are long and interactions with the

Continued

managers are occasionally confrontational since operational managers are frustrated by the endless volume of rules, guidelines, and regulations that surround, in particular, staffing and position classification. Frequently the managers accuse the Human Resources Advisors of being "professional obstructionists" dedicated solely to putting up policy and legislative roadblocks to preclude busy operational managers with stakeholders to satisfy from doing their jobs.

Benjamin McGraw (Ben to his boss and peers, but "Mr. McGraw" to his staff) was an undisputed expert in staffing, classification, and compensation—this knowledge honed over thirty years in the federal government "human resources business", as he likes to refer to it. Ben knew both the rules and the ropes and ran his shop in a way in which he made the decisions and expected his staff to follow his instructions. In McGraw's view, "*Human resources operations is a fast moving and high stress area. Given the range of backgrounds and experience of my staff, it would take days for them to reach consensus on anything and they would miss critical dates. They need rapid and precise direction: what needs to be done, how, when, and where – they needn't worry too much about why.*"

The staff had complete respect for McGraw's expertise and appreciated his clarity in establishing goals, methods, and expectations. In addition to his expertise, he was a confident manager, never doubting his own abilities or his own counsel. His power, among other things was legitimate in that it flowed directly from his position and his employees were not the type to challenge or question his direction. His team was focused on achieving organizational goals established unilaterally by him and had a high need for achievement. Many staff members were inexperienced and needed clarity and guidance to do their work. As well, many of the tasks performed by different employees, while highly structured in some ways, were interdependent: for example, staffing and compensation are inextricably linked.

When McGraw retired, he was replaced by James Donohue, affectionately referred to as *JD*. JD was a generalist, having served in numerous roles throughout DRP and other government departments. JD was self-described as a "people's prince" and embraced a philosophy that he described, in his own words: *"Management is simply getting the right things done through other people. If I can manage the people, I don't need any expertise in anything. People are the most important resource – if you support your people, you will accomplish your organizational goals."*

Indeed JD had a good track record as a manager—objectives had almost always been achieved and employees loved his supportive leadership style. So when he had the opportunity to take over the Human Resources Directorate at DRP, he jumped at it. And true to form he was far from being an expert in any human resource areas, other than having served as an operational manager in several capacities and could, therefore, certainly empathize with his new clients (many of whom were his colleagues as operational managers).

Recognizing his technical shortcomings, JD immediately reorganized the unit so that the most senior staff member (in terms of level) in each area was given the title "manager" and reported directly to him, with others in the respective units reporting to the managers. He now had five direct reports (Staffing, Classification, Labour Relations, Compensation, and Planning), plus his Administrative Assistant. He wanted to develop these people as managers and focused on helping them develop their skills and abilities. He also took a very different tact from McGraw: His managers were responsible for managing their units and this, of course, included responsibility for the necessary technical expertise. When decisions had to be made, all "files" would go to the respective manager who would review the details and develop options and an opinion on the matter, providing a briefing to JD who would ultimately make an "informed" decision—very

Continued

rarely opting for a course of action that differed from the recommended "option."

JD invested in his managers, developing learning plans that offered opportunity to remain abreast of the most current practices at a technical level, but also included "management" and "leadership" courses through which his managers could develop skills necessary to progress beyond managing their small units.

Notwithstanding his investment in his managers, JD insisted on developing a culture permeating throughout the entire directorate that was friendly and encouraging, considerate and understanding, sympathetic, trusting, and respectful. He challenged all his staff to think of ways in which we can help the client—in his words: "...instead of telling clients, 'you can't do that!' tell them what they can do and how you can help them do what they are trying to do."

JD operated an "open-door" policy that extended to every staff member regardless of level. While not a technical expert in any of the managers' areas, he had highly developed interpersonal skills and was a highly skilled communicator. The loyalty of his past staff was legendary and his power was primarily referent. Within weeks of his arrival, his boss was hearing word from clients on how much more helpful Human Resources Directorate seems to be.

Questions:

What type of leadership style was display by Benjamin McGraw and was this style of leadership appropriate? Support your position.

What type of leadership style was displayed by James Donohue? Support your position.

How successful do you feel Donohue's leadership style will be?

The first observation is that this case study, while requiring responses to specific questions, is somewhat longer than a typical short "vignette." In applying steps 1 to 4 above, it can be reasonably surmised that the requirements involve matters of leadership, more specifically, leadership styles, and with even more precision, changing leadership styles in a particular organizational culture that has remained static for years. With this in mind, the case can be reproduced with the "relevant components" highlighted.

Leadership in Human Resources Operations at DRP

The Department of Rare Plants (DRP) is a large, complex federal government department. Many employees are scientists while others are naturalists, and paramilitary types whose job is to ensure the safety and security of naturally occurring rare plants across the country. The mandate of DRP also extends to plants found in ocean beds and shoals occurring to the full extent of the 200 mile exclusive economic zone as well as freshwater lake beds (including the Great Lakes). Many of the employees at DRP have worked in the department for years. The culture is a supportive one with employees genuinely caring about one another and most managers are supportive.

The Human Resources Directorate consists of twenty-five employees headed by Benjamin McGraw who served, until recently, as the Director of this unit for over eight years. Benjamin was sixty years old and had spent his entire career in Human Resources, starting as a staffing officer "back in the day" when it was called "Personnel."

This directorate is very operational. It is concerned with staffing, compensation, training, and labour relations and providing these services to 7,000 employees. The nature of this work generally involves applying a

Continued

plethora of policies and guidelines to human resources requests made by operational managers. As such there is always a need to interpret policies made by Central Agencies and apply this interpretation to the actions being proposed by operational managers.

Of the twenty-five staff, most are employees at junior levels of the personnel administration classification group—PE-02 or PE-03. McGraw himself is a PE-06 (the most senior level in this category). The employees typically are young and have varying degrees of expertise and experience, despite being at the same classification level. This is partly to do with practice of promoting employees quickly in order to reduce turnover (if you don't promote them, some other department will), as PE employees are in shortage in the federal government, and partly due to varying practices and expectations in different departments. For example, in small departments and agencies, a PE-02 or PE-03 might be expected to provide a broader range of services, becoming more of a generalist than a specialist. For the employees of the Human Resources Directorate, the days are long and interactions with the managers are occasionally confrontational since operational managers are frustrated by the endless volume of rules, guidelines, and regulations that surround, in particular, staffing and position classification. Frequently the managers accuse the Human Resources Advisors of being "professional obstructionists" dedicated solely to putting up policy and legislative roadblocks to preclude busy operational managers with stakeholders to satisfy from doing their jobs.

Benjamin McGraw (Ben to his boss and peers, but "Mr. McGraw" to his staff) was an undisputed expert in staffing, classification, and compensation—this knowledge honed over thirty years in the federal government "human resources business, as he likes to refer to it." Ben knew both the rules and the ropes and ran his shop in a way in which he made the decisions and expected his staff to follow his instructions. In McGraw's view, "*Human resources operations is a fast moving and high stress area. Given the range of backgrounds and experience of my staff, it would take days for them to reach consensus on any-thing and they would miss critical dates. They need rapid and precise direction: what needs to be done, how, when, and where – they needn't worry too much about why."*

The staff had complete respect for McGraw's expertise and appreci-ated his clarity in establishing goals, methods, and expectations. In addition to his expertise, he was a confident manager, never doubting his own abilities or his own counsel. His power, among other things was legitimate in that it flowed directly from his position and his employees were not the type to challenge or question his direction. His team was focused on achieving organizational goals established unilaterally by him and had a high need for achievement. Many staff members were inexperienced and needed clarity and guidance to do their work. As well, many of the tasks performed by different employ-ees, while highly structured in some ways, were interdependent: for example, staffing and compensation are inextricably linked.

When McGraw retired, he was replaced by James Donohue, affection-ately referred to as *JD*. JD was a generalist, having served in numer-ous roles throughout DRP and other government departments. JD was self-described as a "people's prince" and embraced a philosophy that he described, in his own words: *"Management is simply getting the right things done through other people. If I can manage the people, I don't need any expertise in anything. People are the most important resource – if you support your people, you will accomplish your orga-nizational goals."*

Indeed JD had a good track record as a manager—objectives had almost always been achieved and employees loved his supportive leadership style. So when he had the opportunity to take over the Human Resources Directorate at DRP, he jumped at it. And true to form he was far from being an expert in any human resource areas, other than having served as an operational manager in several

Continued

capacities and could, therefore, certainly empathize with his new clients (many of whom were his colleagues as operational managers).

Recognizing his technical shortcomings, JD immediately reorganized the unit so that the most senior staff member (in terms of level) in each area was given the title "manager" and reported directly to him, with others in the respective units reporting to the managers. He now had five direct reports (Staffing, Classification, Labour Relations, Compensation, and Planning), plus his Administrative Assistant. He wanted to develop these people as managers and focused on helping them develop their skills and abilities. He also took a very different tact from McGraw: His managers were responsible for managing their units and this, of course, included responsibility for the necessary technical expertise. When decisions had to be made, all "files" would go to the respective manager who would review the details and develop options and an opinion on the matter, providing a briefing to JD who would ultimately make an "informed" decision—very rarely opting for a course of action that differed from the recommended "option."

JD invested in his managers, developing learning plans that offered opportunity to remain abreast of the most current practices at a technical level, but also included "management" and "leadership" courses through which his managers could develop skills necessary to progress beyond managing their small units.

Notwithstanding his investment in his managers, JD insisted on developing a culture permeating throughout the entire directorate that was friendly and encouraging, considerate and understanding, sympathetic, trusting, and respectful. He challenged all his staff to think of ways in which we can help the client—in his words: "...instead of telling clients, 'you can't do that!' tell them what they can do and how you can help them do what they are trying to do."

JD operated an "open-door" policy that extended to every staff member regardless of level. While not a technical expert in any of the managers' areas, he had highly developed interpersonal skills and was a highly skilled communicator. The loyalty of his past staff was legendary and his power was primarily referent. Within weeks of his arrival, his boss was hearing word from clients on how much more helpful Human Resources Directorate seems to be.

Questions:

What type of leadership style was displayed by Benjamin McGraw and was this style of leadership appropriate? Support your position.

What type of leadership style was displayed by James Donohue? Support your position.

How successful do you feel Donohue's leadership style will be?

As you contemplate Step 5 (from Page 12), the next consideration would be whether any of the previously identified components of the environment of organizations (Figure 1 from Page 3) are explicit in this case study, and if so, the extent to which they require explicit treatment in developing the responses to the case questions. Most obviously this involves *people* and an appreciation for the *organizational culture* prevailing at the level of the Human Resources Directorate, the "headset" of department managers and their view of Human Resources (i.e., "professional obstructionists," and the overall prevailing culture of the department itself. The cultural representatives of each of these identified groups are also *stakeholders*. Less obvious and less relevant to this particular case, the practice of human resources must be *ethical* (who gets hired, for example) and whether public sector or private sector, the human resources' function is expensive and therefore involves *money*. It is important to note that the goal is not to "force fit" every component to every case—in this particular case example as is typical with this style of case study (where specific questions are provided) the focus should be on the subject matter at hand. That said, let's work toward developing a response to this case study.

There are a number of factors at play in this case, that should be "teased out" as we consider a response to each of the questions:

- What is leadership?
- What styles of leadership are described in the literature, and of these styles, which style is exemplified by McGraw and James Donohue?
- What is organizational culture?
- How would you describe the prevailing organizational culture in the Human Resources Branch?
- What is the relationship between the organizational culture in the Human Resources Branch and the view of operational managers and the overall department?
- What is power?
- What is meant by legitimate power and referent power?
- What is organizational change?
- Will the change in leadership constitute an organizational change?

In considering the two questions on leadership style, there are two important factors: (1) to define what leadership is, and (2) to describe the prevailing "leadership styles" in the literature. Clearly a fully developed response to the two questions necessarily requires a demonstration that the writer understands what s/he is talking about. If you don't present a definition of leadership, do you truly understand what it is? If you don't present the key prevailing leadership theories, how does the reader know your selected style represents a "fully informed" selection? Now, regarding answering the case questions…

> What type of leadership style was displayed by Benjamin McGraw and was this style of leadership appropriate? Support your position.

A response that would **not** meet expectations would be as follows:

McGraw is a directive leader because he has a need to give orders and tightly control the actions of his subordinates.

Another response that would **not** meet expectations would be as follows:

After having undertaken considerable background research that appears in the appendix to this case, it is clear that McGraw is a directive leader because he has a need to give orders and tightly control the actions of his subordinates.

Why do these not meet expectations? There are several reasons however I have found that the most effective way to explain to students the shortcomings of their answer is to provide what would be perceived as an excellent response.

Consider this response that would *at least* "fully meet" expectations; starting with some background secondary research that will be mined when constructing the answer to each question:

There are several areas of study that are germane to responding to the questions in this case. These areas will be considered as backgrounds used in formulating the response to the questions.

First, **leadership** for which there are several definitions, one of which is *"the ability to direct or inspire people to reach goals."*[1] In addition to common goals, leadership has also been presented by some authors as a *process* that involves *influence.*[2]

Leadership styles run the spectrum ranging from autocratic at one extreme to free-rein leadership at the other extreme. For the purpose of this case study, the core leadership styles proposed as leadership behaviors by Howell and Costley can represent target points on this spectrum[3]:

Directive leaders set goals, define roles, make decisions, and communicate these decisions to subordinates. Directive leaders can become closely controlling, authoritarian, and autocratic.

Supportive leaders show concern for and interest in, subordinates, promote open communications, show trust and respect, and invest in their professional development.

Participative leaders involve subordinates in making decisions, demonstrate integrity and empathy, and listen effectively.

Charismatic leaders are perceived as "having exceptional (almost magical) qualities that inspire extreme devotion, commitment, and trust."[4] Among other traits, charismatic leaders are strong role models…appear competent…exhibit confidence of follower's abilities to meet expectations…and arouse task-relevant motives.[5]

---

[1] Boone, Kurtz, Khan,Canzer: *Conteporary Business Second Canadian Edition.* John Wiley and Sons Canada, Ltd., 2016, 193.

[2] Northouse, Peter G.: *Leadership Theory and Practice*, Fifth Edition. Sage Publications Inc.,2010 3.

[3] Howell, Jon P., and Dan L. Costley.: *Understanding Behaviors for Effective Leadership*, Second Edition. Pearson Education Inc., 2006.

[4] Ibid. p.209

[5] Northouse, Peter G.: *Leadership Theory and Practice*, Fifth Edition. Sage Publications Inc., 2010, 174–75.

While many models of leadership exist in the literature, it is important to note that no single leadership style will fit every situation and leaders who are able to change leadership styles to suit prevailing circumstances are rare. It is therefore, possible for the same leader to exhibit different styles: for example, the same leader could be both supportive and directive.

Author's Note: The information above sets the stage for responding to the leadership component of questions 1 and 3. Leadership has been defined and an approach to describing leadership style(s) has been provided (there are other possible approaches to leadership style that are perfectly acceptable, however, having read the question(s) and hopefully having a general idea of an approach to the response, it is best to select an approach that in which your response can be appropriately anchored— based on the characteristics of the "leaders" portrayed in the case. In addition, the background draws from secondary sources which are fully cited, respecting scholarship.

Second, **power**—any style of leadership requires having a degree of power. Power generally refers to one person's ability to influence another person to do something. Power can stem from many sources including, but not limited to, a person's position in an organizational hierarchy (legitimate, reward, and coercive), a person's charismatic aura (referent), or a person's level of expertise (expert).

Legitimate power arises from a person's position—as the "holder" of a "senior position," for example, the person has the right to make the request of other persons who have the obligation to comply—but could also arise from a person's "expertise" in a field.

Referent power arises from "followers" wanting to imitate a person with whom they identify.

Third, **organizational culture**—"a system of shared meaning and beliefs held by organizational members that determines, in large degree, how they act toward each other and outsiders."[6]

There are many dimensions of organizational culture including, among others, attention to detail, people orientation, aggressiveness, and stability.[7]

Fourth, **organizational change**—"*any alteration of people, structure, or technology in an organization.*"[8] A change in people can result in changes to prevailing expectations, attitudes, and behaviors.[9]

Author's Note: Power, organizational culture, and organizational change have a significant impact on leadership. It is necessary to consider these factors in a situation in which a change of leadership is occurring.

Now, the responses to the questions:

> What type of leadership style was displayed by Benjamin McGraw and was this style of leadership appropriate? Support your position.

Based on the leadership styles selected, McGraw demonstrates directive leadership behaviour. This is supported by the manner in which he "ran his shop"—he made the decisions and expected his staff to follow his instructions; articulating what needed to be done, how, when, and where; without concern for his staff understanding or learning "why." The goals for his unit were established by him, without

---

[6] Robbins, Coulter, Leach, and Kilfoil: *Management*, Twelfth Edition. Pearson Canada Inc., 2019, 38.

[7] Ibid. p.39

[8] Ibid. p.171

[9] Ibid.

input from his staff. McGraw appeared to be closely controlling. In addition to close control, McGraw demonstrated authoritarian and autocratic tendencies: "Ben to his boss and peers, but "Mr. McGraw" to his staff. McGraw's power is sourced from two areas: (1) his position and (2) his expertise; these legitimate power sources could feed and support his directive leadership behavior, and his apparent unwillingness to invest in developing his staff (teaching the "why") would further solidify the continuation of his "expertise" without challenge.

The appropriateness of any style of leadership is influenced by several variables, among them organizational culture, the nature of the work, and the capacity of organizational staff. The nature of the work is policy and guidelines-centric, complicated, and a continuous effort to interpret policies. The capacity of the staff members is portrayed as minimal with many inexperienced staff performing tasks that were interdependent. Furthermore, to reduce turnover, there is a tendency to promote staff before they are ready to assume the duties and responsibilities of higher-level positions. Organizational culture as represented by a system of shared meaning and beliefs determining how they act toward each other and outsiders, could be described as one in which attention to detail prevails against a backdrop of instability (staff turnover), occasional aggressiveness in terms of interaction with some operational managers. While it is tempting to suggest a lack of people orientation, this is not entirely supported by the case study content—the staff had complete respect for McGraw's expertise and appreciated his clarity. The combination of the nature of the work, the inexperience of the staff, and the prevailing organizational culture would tend to suggest that *a certain degree* of directive leadership would be necessary. Demonstrating some supportive leader tendencies such as, for example, investing in staff professional development, could effectively complement the directive leadership style, and possibly provoke an organizational cultural change that would over time, reduce the need for an autocratic directive leadership approach.

Author's Note: You will note the application of the earlier concepts "teased out" as "Background." This approach assists in developing an answer to a question that is built upon a particularly compelling foundation. The response is appropriate, logical, and supported by both examples extracted from the case study as well as theoretical constructs.

> What type of leadership style was displayed by James Donohue? Support your position.

The leadership style displayed by James Donohue would most certainly <u>not</u> fit the description of autocratic, authoritarian, or any degree of directive. His style emanates characteristics of supportive and participative styles, and leans toward charismatic. In arriving at a dominant style, it is necessary to consider some practical observations concerning James' approach from the case:

- People-centric (people are the most important resource)
- A focus on staff development to facilitate progression to higher levels
- Participative decision-making
- An open-door policy
- Highly developed interpersonal skills and an effective communicator
- Staff loyalty, commitment, and trust

These observations would suggest a style beyond showing concern, being friendly, and considerate, and helps in their aspirations (supportive); and consulting with managers (who presumably consult with their subordinates) on matters requiring decisions prior to *making* the decision clearly suggests a participative leadership approach. But James also appears to have a strong track record of followers exhibiting devotion, commitment, and trust. James appears to have considerable strength in his conviction in his ideas and beliefs, and notwithstanding his lack of subject matter expertise, he demonstrates considerable self-confidence and self-assurance through his assertive activities to reorganize and appoint managers. His power appears to be derived from his "people's prince" practices of establishing loyalty, commitment, and trust through a range of different roles in other government departments—suggesting referent power. Taken collectively, this would support the view that James was a charismatic leader.

How successful do you feel Donohue's leadership style will be?

Substituting a directive leader with expert power with a charismatic leader with referent power in an operational environment characterized by high turnover of inexperienced staff dealing with endless rules, guidelines, and regulations, and an organization generally perceived by a number of clients as "professional obstructionists" is a monumental undertaking. Donohue is not a subject matter expert, and therefore success will be a function of how effectively and efficiently he can implement an organizational change (people—himself as leader;

structure—new management roles; behaviours—open door and team approach), an organizational culture change, and engender the level of trust from staff in his ability to undertake supportive activities while simultaneously ensuring that operations continue to operate effectively.

Among other things, Donohue will need to exude confidence in himself and his staff regarding his vision, consistently "walk the talk" in being considerate, understanding, sympathetic, trustful, and respectful in order to change the organizational culture, and invest in staff personal training and development to reduce turnover. Creating an organization from which staff are reluctant to leave will be a necessary goal. These several objectives are attainable, but will take time and Donohue will need to rely on his experience in other organizations — what worked, what didn't work—to bring this high-risk assignment to a successful conclusion.

Author's Note: This final question is seeking your opinion and as such, the responses are many and varied. The approach taken is to characterize the scenario in which Donohue is entering, followed by some recommendations on what he would need to do to be successful.

Toward a Grading Rubric

It should be obvious why this most recent response is superior to the earlier response portrayed as "not meeting expectations." This nomenclature deserves explanation. Expectations reflect what the professor "expects" to be found in an acceptable response and is determined by individual professors/instructors based on any number of factors including, but not limited to, the class time spent on certain concepts, the level of research, and other factors. Generally, the following categories are instructive:

Category	Explanation
Does Not Meet Expectations	There are a number of key concepts missing or given minimal/marginal treatment
Meets Most Expectations	The key concepts are covered, although not in appropriate depth
Fully Meets Expectations	The key concepts are covered in appropriate depth
Exceeds Expectations	The key concepts are thoroughly covered to a level that demonstrates "going above and beyond" to include, for example, a (secondary) research effort that links theoretical constructs directly to the case, presenting a particularly compelling position on the matter at hand

Applying this structure to the DRP case is particularly instructive. Note that professors and instructors may have different views on the appropriateness of what constitutes a response that falls into each of the above categories (but I expect there would be general concurrence on the content of a response that "Does Not Meet Expectations" ☺).

A suggested general guiding rubric is provided on the following page. The description is "general" by design, recognizing that grading a case study is a subjective exercise. Rubrics can also be made more explicit and reflect letter grade ranges as portrayed on Page 34, applied to question 1 of the DRP case. Note that case studies are graded typically using a rubric that articulates content expectations, but also *relative* to all other cases submitted.

Associated General Guiding Rubric—DPR Case Questions

Parameter	Exceeds Expectations A+	Fully Meets Expectations A, A-, B+, B	Meets Most Expectations C+, C, D+, D	Does Not Meet Expectations F
Calibre of the **Content** of the Written Response	The response reflects considerable effort to define key concepts and "models" that will directly impact on the response, and these definitions are sourced from multiple sources that could include academic journals and/or from practitioners	The response reflects a reasonable effort to define key concepts and "models" that will directly impact on the response, and these definitions are sourced from the course text book and other text books	The response reflects some effort to define key concepts and "models" that will directly impact on the response, but some applicable concepts have not been considered and those definitions and models that are included are taken from the course text book or online sources	The response does not define key concepts; there is no effort to consult other sources of information
	The response clearly links the key concepts and models to the position of the writer so the reader is convinced of the logic of the argument in all respects	The response links the key concepts and models to the position of the writer so the reader is convinced of the logic of the argument in most respects	The response links the key concepts and models considered to the position of the writer but the reader is not always convinced of the logic of the argument	The response is a very minimal effort with many aspects missing
	The content represents a perfect balance between information that informs the response, and the response itself	The content represents a good balance between information that informs the response, and the response itself		

Associated General Guiding Rubric—DPR Case Questions   (continued)

Parameter	Exceeds Expectations A+	Fully Meets Expectations A, A-, B+, B	Meets Most Expectations C+, C, D+, D	Does Not Meet Expectations F
Calibre of the Written Response	The response is completely free of spelling and grammatical errors The response is exceptionally well written and organized, demonstrating considerable effort and attention to quality Citations are used appropriately	The response is for the most part free of spelling and grammatical errors The response is reasonably well written and organized, demonstrating effort and attention to quality Citations are used appropriately	The response contains spelling and grammatical errors that reflect insufficient attention to detail in proofreading The response is not particularly well written although it is possible to follow the argument in most cases Citations are used appropriately, with minor formatting issues noted	The response is fraught with grammatical and spelling errors, is poorly written, poorly organized, and demonstrates neither effort nor attention to quality

Associated Specific Guiding Rubric—DPR Case Question 1

What type of leadership style was displayed by Benjamin McGraw and was this style of leadership appropriate? Support your position.

Parameter	Exceeds Expectations A+	Fully Meets Expectations A, A-, B+, B	Meets Most Expectations C+, C, D+, D	Does Not Meet Expectations F
Calibre of the **Content** of the Written Response	Leadership is fully defined Possible leadership styles are described and discussed (egs.): • Directive • Supportive • Participative • Charismatic Other factors that influence leadership are described and discussed (egs.): • Power • Organizational culture • Organizational change The response draws from these factors, sourced from several sources, in supporting the position that McGraw is a directive leader	Leadership is fully defined Possible leadership styles are described and discussed, but not in the same detail as a response that "exceeds" The model(s) of leadership styles selected may not always dovetail with the direction of the response, but the logic of the response is sound Many of the factors that influence leadership are described and discussed, and these are an appropriate match to the response The response concludes that McGraw is a directive leader	Leadership is defined but the response does not adequately explore all possible leadership styles that could apply to the case—the leadership style that is presumed to be predominant—directive leadership—is described and discussed Many of the factors that influence leadership are not sufficiently described or discussed The response concludes that McGraw is a directive leader	Leadership is not defined Leadership styles are not described or discussed There is weak or little or non-existent support for the style of leadership exhibited by McGraw—simply a statement of the style of leadership exhibited with no support for the position taken.

Associated Specific Guiding Rubric—DPR Case Question 1

What type of leadership style was displayed by Benjamin McGraw and was this style of leadership appropriate? Support your position.   (continued)

Parameter	Exceeds Expectations A+	Fully Meets Expectations A, A-, B+, B	Meets Most Expectations C+, C, D+, D	Does Not Meet Expectations F
Calibre of the Written Response	The response is completely free of spelling and grammatical errors The response is exceptionally well written and organized, demonstrating considerable effort and attention to quality Citations are used appropriately	The response is for the most part free of spelling and grammatical errors The response is reasonably well written and organized, demonstrating effort and attention to quality Citations are used appropriately	The response contains spelling and grammatical errors that reflect insufficient attention to detail in proofreading The response is not particularly well written although it is possible to follow the argument in most cases Citations are used appropriately, with minor formatting issues noted	The response is fraught with grammatical and spelling errors, is poorly written, poorly organized, and demonstrates neither effort nor attention to quality

A Case to Explore

Before moving on to the next style of case studies—those without specific questions, consider applying the approach presented above to the following case.

Dr. Larry Miller and the Manure Enzyme [10]

Larry Miller (aka Doc Larry) was a researcher at an obscure university in northern Canada. His research focused on ways in which certain enzymes could modify petroleum products such that they could be used for fertilizers. There was of course great potential in this research—including, but not limited to "greening" oil spills and discarded old gasoline and used motor oil—but very little political will to invest in his research. Dr. Lawrence Milfred Michael Millar held two earned doctorates—one in chemical engineering and other in biotechnology. Well qualified and widely published, his theories were somewhat radical and presented a significant political risk to local politicians who may otherwise have been inclined to support his research with taxpayers' money.

Doc Larry was undaunted by this lack of political support and researched tirelessly in areas of enzymes. One morning on his hobby farm, Larry accidentally spilled some Enzyme QM on an open bag of sheep manure he used to fertilize his several gardens. The chemical reaction was instantaneous and amazing—the resulting liquid, when tested, presented identical properties as *91 octane gasoline* and further testing indicated that it could be used as a very clean burning fuel in any gasoline combustion engine: cleaner even than ethanol!

---

[10] Note: This case previously appeared as "Crazy Larry and the Manure Enzyme" in Delcorde, David H.J.: Canadian Business and Society, Kendall Hunt Publishing Company (2013).

Doc Larry immediately registered his intellectual property under scientific patent and called the "product" *LM*. He then established a private corporation, bringing in some of his scientific colleagues—Barry, Harry, and Garry as both shareholders and managers of LM Incorporated (**LMI**). Larry of course held 51 percent of the shares so he had both legal and effective control of the company.

For five years **LMI** perfected the product and streamlined the manufacturing process. Larry offered up much of his farmland to neighbours as a dumping zone for, well, let's say manure of all types. But despite the bounty of manure, he soon realized that to make **LMI** a commercially viable venture, a factory approach would be necessary, and this would require considerably more money than Larry, Barry, Harry, and Garry could pull together. The business plan predicted an enormous international market for this feces fuel as it could be virtually substituted for gasoline, manufactured for a fraction of the cost, and run in any engine—with slight modification to the formula, research had demonstrated it could even burn in jet engines and the engines of the Space Shuttles. In spite of the tremendous financial gains, it would make enormous contributions to greening the environment and reducing greenhouse gas production.

To get more money, many options existed—angel investors, government investment, a public offering of **LMI** shares, among others. Larry decided to take **LMI** public and in six months had sold enough shares to have more than enough capital to establish a commercially viable feces-fuel-producing factory that would meet or exceed all the profit projections in the business plan—the same projections that were part of the prospectus sent to brokers through which to entice investment in the company. This was the good news: the bad news was now he only controlled about 20 percent of the voting shares; Barry, Harry, and Garry now owned about 5 percent each. The single largest block investor was the Northern Canadian Pension Fund that

Continued

controlled 35 percent of the voting shares. The remaining 30 percent of the shares were widely held with no single investor owning significant holdings.

Late one evening, shortly before the grand opening of the **LMI** manufacturing facility, Harry and Garry were looking over the results of some related scientific experiments. They were astounded to discover that when the modified feces fuel "LM" was combined with erythromycin and injected into rats presenting with a malignant tumour growth, not only did the cancerous growth stop, it disappeared completely within a week. This was an important discovery— one that had the potential of virtually wiping out several different types of cancer. Pleased with their discovery, they met with Larry and Barry. All four scientists were thrilled with the potential of this discovery, but their euphoria soon evaporated as they thought this through.

The prospectus and agreement with the investors, in particular the Northern Canada Pension Fund, guaranteed investors that the LM would only be used for the production of feces fuel with no other applications for a period of ten years. The agreement further stipulated that all scientific work on the LM would be directed to making efficiency and effectiveness gains in production, distribution, and application of the LM. Moreover, the corporation **LMI**, not Larry, owned the patent on the LM.

The scientists considered their options.

Questions:

Who are the key stakeholders in this case and what are their stakes?

In your view, how would you attempt to resolve this "ethical dilemma"?

Some background considerations in developing your responses:

- What is stakeholder?
- What is key stakeholder?
- What models of stakeholder analysis are available, through which you could develop a defensible list of "key" stakeholders?
- What is ethics?
- What is an ethical dilemma?
- Which components that collectively comprise the environment of organizations as discussed on page 4 are relevant in this case:
  - People
  - Stakeholders
  - Money
  - Ethics
  - Social Responsibility?

Style 2—Cases that Require "Open-Ended Responses"

Most instructors that I know would perceive this style of case as more difficult. The style of open-ended "question" can take many forms: *Advise the Chief Executive; prepare a response to the allegation; would you agree with the position taken by the Minister of Precious Minerals? What would you do?* This requires considerably more analysis in determining the primary problem, secondary problem(s), constraints, assumptions, impact on people, stakeholders, money, ethics, and social responsibility, in arriving at a solution (or response, or recommendation).

There is a fine line between a detailed analysis and a *fulsome* analysis, and determining the correct amount is an art learned over time, after undertaking many case analyses. Be aware that it is fine to use appendices provided the contents support the analysis—it is not fine to use appendices as an excuse to avoid writing: for example, writing something like, "*as supported by the material in the appendix, McGraw's leadership style is clearly directive,*" is not fine! Some realities of this type of case analysis are worth noting. Every case does not require the analysis of every conceivable subject matter area—care and rigor must be used to carefully select those areas germane to the case, and develop the concepts appropriately. As well, this type of case while typically longer than those requiring responses to specific questions, do not have to be long to be complicated.

In dealing with this style of case study, it is instructive to provide some guidance on a general approach, noting that any suggested approach will not always work in all cases—welcome to the world of case analysis! The most effective way to evolving an "approach" is to demonstrate its development through an analysis of an actual case. We will do this using the case found below (SEM), however, before embarking on this exercise it is instructive to follow the initial steps from page 12, reproduced here:

1. Read the case thoroughly before considering the actual requirements;

2. Read the requirements;

3. Read the case again, with the requirements in mind, and highlight what you feel are the relevant components;

4. Compare what you have highlighted with the requirements; and

5. Think about how you would approach responding to the case requirements.

For this style of case, the requirements are much vaguer than for cases featuring specific questions. It is therefore critical at the outset to determine, as precisely as possible, what you are required to do, what role are you playing for example. In the case that follows, you are required to *"Advise Martin Black on a recommended course of action"* and you must, therefore keep this in mind at all times. Further, this particular case while initially appearing somewhat straightforward is, in reality, anything but! It will be necessary to develop the correct focus on the correct aspects of the case that will influence and support your recommended course of action. You should also bear in mind that any recommended course of action must be realistic, and the better case analyses approaches will require some verbiage on how you would implement the recommendation. The proposed implementation must also be realistic! For example, doubling the staff and quadrupling the budget may certainly solve the primary problem but is completely unrealistic given any "real-world" constraints!

Let's now consider the SEM case below; you will do steps 1, 2, 4, and 5; I have already done step 3 (which you may or may not agree with—up to you—but I *am* the author ☺).

Smith's Electric Motorcycles Inc. (SEM)[11]

In 2019, Martin Black joined Smith's Electric Motorcycles Inc. (SEM) as Director of Marketing and Customer Relations. Black was well qualified as an electrical engineer with an MBA and several years' experience in marketing and applied science. Given the movement

Continued

---

[11] This case is inspired by *"An Explosive Problem at Gigantic Motors"*, written by John Haas of the George Mason University.

toward electric vehicles catalyzed by environmental concerns and a growing public demeanour toward environmental protection, Black felt that SEM was developing and promoting the electric motorcycle at the perfect time.

Black's main responsibility was to expand the market for Smith's newest offering, branded the "Electric Jet"—an electric motorcycle that offered the same performance as most 750 to 850 cc gasoline-powered motorcycles offered by the competition. This was not Smith's first offering: SEM had offered the "Smith Electric Cruiser" since 2010 and this electric motorcycle had been well received by the market. Two common complaints were that it was underpowered and required a full eight-hour charge to obtain a range of 250 kilometres. The Electric Jet would resolve these problems by offering a full charge time period of three hours and a range of 500 kilometres on a full charge. As the Electric Jet was based on the Smith Electric Cruiser platform, some redesigning would be necessary.

During the course of redesigning the Electric Cruiser to become the Electric Jet, Black joined the two production and design engineers in reviewing all the old schematics used in the design of the Electric Cruiser, as well as all the accident reports on hand. Black noted that the battery packs were mounted to the frame using rubber grommets (sourced from an offshore company) intended to buffer vibrations and reduce potential rattling, as well as to serve as insulation against potential electric shock cause by metal-to-metal contact. This had worked so well on the Electric Cruiser that the design for the Electric Jet used the same system, with two additional mounting points to compensate for the heavier battery packs required in order to meet the performance targets of the Electric Jet.

At first, this design appeared entirely reasonable: the batteries were well secured and the approach required no modifications beyond the minor addition of two additional rubber grommets. This would save production time and money. As Black reviewed the accident reports on hand for the Electric Cruiser since 2010, he noted that of the thirty accidents for which the company had information, twenty-eight were attributed, either directly or indirectly, to fire, generally caused by failure of the battery packs. A more detailed examination indicated that the battery pack failure was not only a result of a collision or a drop (which would certainly explain the resulting fire caused by the ignition of the battery pack from shorting out). Some accidents were also caused by what appeared to be the simultaneous ignition of the battery packs while the Electric Cruiser was being ridden, *prior to* the collision or drop. Further analysis revealed an issue of "rubber grommet fatigue" caused by fluctuations in temperature and lack of use: factors typically at play during the winter months when motorcycles are typically stored, and rarely in temperature-controlled environments. Of the twenty-eight accidents, twenty-five could be directly attributed to rubber grommet fatigue.

Black raised the issue with Michael Martin, the chief engineer, who had served with SEM since its inception in 1995, pointing out that unlike most automobiles, motorcycles last for years with much of their time spent in storage. As a result, the rubber grommet fatigue was likely rampant and SEM had "just been lucky" that no one had attributed the fires to a design flaw. Black also emphasized that SEM has a responsibility to not only modify the design on the Electric Jet, but also recall any and all, Electric Cruisers in use and modify the design, as the current design is clearly a safety issue. Black was adamant about the need to raise this with the CEO and the Board of Directors.

Michael Martin's reaction was swift: "Martin, first of all there have been no incidences of death or legal inquiries arising from any of the reports you analyzed. Second, the twenty-eight accident reports collectively represent less than 1 percent of the sold units of the Electric Jet over the years. Third, the costs involved in a modification to the Electric

Continued

Jet's mounting system would significantly erode the already slim profit margins we are working with, not to mention the unimaginable costs involved in a recall of all Electric Jets that would likely bankrupt the company. Furthermore, if this gets out, the competition would slaughter us!! Leave it alone Martin! This is a minor matter and not worth opening a can of worms."

Black considered his options.

Required:

Advise Martin Black on a recommended course of action.

Where to begin?

As a starting point, consider the "subject matters" that are at play in this case. In no particular order, I would suggest the following:

- Electric vehicles are excellent for the environment but they must also be safe (people)
- Stakeholders
- Money (profit margins, costs)
- Ethics
- Globalization: rubber grommets sourced from an offshore company

What is the primary problem?

Your recommended course of action will address the primary problem. In my view, the primary problem is: Martin Black has discovered that SEM has sold, and plans to sell, a product with potential defects that could harm people and must decide, in the absence of support from the design team, whether to raise this matter directly with the CEO and the Board of Directors.

In the perfect world, a primary problem can be reduced to one specific issue, however this depends on the case. In contrast, secondary problems are defined by some writers as either a cause or a result of the primary problem. An interesting test of the reliability of your selection of the primary problem is to consider what happens when the primary problem goes away. There is, then, no case. For example, one could argue that if Black did not become aware of the problem, it would still exist but no one would know about it, ergo no problem.

Having defined the primary problem for which a recommendation on a course of action to deal with it is required, we can now consider some of the factors that are in play, the development of which is required in progressing a response.

Author's Note: As with the first case style examined, this background can be contained in an appendix—but the salient points must be brought into the written response: Do not make oversimplified statements, or statements that are not fully developed, and refer to the appendix as your magical "catch all" for detail. The appendix is a support document, not a substitute for the written case response!

Stakeholders

Stakeholders as a concept is intuitively simple—a stakeholder can be described as any person or organization that has a perceived direct or indirect interest in the activities of, in this instance, SEM. With this in mind, it is a relatively simple task to elaborate a list of "stakeholders"—but this is not good enough. The neat thing about stakeholders is that a stakeholder can be anyone or anything, many of whom do not truly understand their "stakes." A practical reality of stakeholder analysis is that there will be perceived "winners" and "losers" as it is not possible to meet the needs of every person or every organization with a perceived stake. Occasionally it is informative to try to determine who is not a stakeholder. For example, Uncle Matt's rich granny who lives in a nursing home and no longer has a driver's licence and will never buy an Electric Jet, so she is clearly not a stakeholder—right? The response is, well, perhaps. But what if Uncle Matt's rich granny is willing to buy *him* an Electric Jet, *"provided it's safe."* Is she still a non-stakeholder? Stakeholder analysis is complicated and extremely important. So how can we determine a manageable group of stakeholders?

Consider the concept of "key stakeholders." A *key stakeholder* has the ability to exert and sustain a positive or negative effect on an organization. Although there are many stakeholder mapping models in the literature, a more intuitive model maps stakeholders according to their power to influence the organization, and the extent to which they are likely to show an interest in the activities of the organization. Using this as a guide, key stakeholders could be described as those persons or organizations with **significant power** to influence the organization **and high interest** in the activities of the organization. [12] For SEM, some key stakeholders and their "stake" would include:

- Owners/shareholders of SEM (stake: profit maximization, return on investment (ROI), publicity that could be detrimental to profits and ROI);

---

[12] A. Mendelow. *Proceedings of 2nd International Conference on Information Systems*, Cambridge, MA, 1981. Johnson, Gerry, and Kevan Scholes. *Exploring Corporate Strategy: Text and Cases, 3rd ed..* London: Prentice-Hall International, 176–177, 1993.

- SEM Board of Directors (stake: upholding their fiduciary duty to act in the best interests of the corporation);
- Customers who own Electric Cruisers and those who will purchase Electric Jets (stake: a reliable, safe product);
- Employees of SEM (stake: continuing employment);
- Competition (stake: market share).

Environmental Concerns

There is clearly a movement toward environmental responsibility with many consumers willing to pay a premium for products that are environmentally friendly and not contributing to pollution and global warming. Environmentalists could very much applaud and support the activities of SEM in developing an "environmentally sensitive" product; this group may not be as supportive if the design flaw was known.

Money

SEM is a "for profit" company and as a corporation (Inc.), is owned by shareholders. Shareholders purchase shares (representing ownership) expecting to receive a return on investment commensurate with the level of risk perceived in the investment instrument. The risk-return-trade-off holds that greater return can be expected in higher-risk investments.

For SEM, shareholders have purchased their shares on the basis of a prospectus that would, among other things, portray operational and strategic initiatives that would provide a measure of the risk involved. If, for example, the design flaw issue was made known to the shareholders they may elect to pull their investment judging the potential fallout to be too risky.

Globalization

Globalization, described most frequently as some version of a convergence of markets and interrelated business relationships, enters into this case in a subtle manner: the rubber grommets are sourced from an offshore company. Not much about this is mentioned in the case study but it represents an important element. In the simplest consideration, the rubber grommets in question are not manufactured by SEM, but what does this actually mean? That because of this SEM is not responsible? Hardly! There are many points to be made relating to this observation:

- Sourcing the grommets from an offshore company does not alleviate safety responsibilities from SEM;
- SEM has a responsibility to ensure, frequently, that the offshore manufacturer is producing this product in accordance with the specifications—any deviation from which needs to be corrected or another supplier found, because of the first bullet above;
- Global sourcing of components is pervasive across all industries to benefit from cost reductions on inputs in order to be competitive; failure to source globally could result in a company's inability to compete, particularly where producing the component domestically would be too expensive, or where the manufacturing facilities do not exist.

Ethics

Ethics refer to *rules and principles that define right and wrong behaviour.* [13] As simple as this definition appears, ethics is a complicated landscape. Morals, duty, values, and beliefs factor into what is perceived as right

---

[13] Davis, K., and W.C. Frederick. *Business and Society: Management, Public Policy, Ethics*, 5th ed. New York: McGraw-Hill., pp. 28–41, 1984.

and wrong behavior, and these are influenced by many factors including culture, organizational leaders, and media. The issue before Martin Black, that comprises an important component of the key issue in the case, is the need to make a decision that concerns a matter of ethics, taking into account the impact of this decision on key stakeholders. In essence, the question before Martin is whether to raise the matter to the CEO or the Board of Directors. In order to arrive at this decision, a number of considerations are at play:

- Are the findings of his analysis correct and reliable, beyond a reasonable doubt?
- Is it ethical for the company to do nothing?
- Is it the right course of action to raise this matter with senior management, recognizing the potential negative impacts that would occur if word got out?
- On a personal level, Martin Black must decide:
  - Is the decision to "blow the whistle"
    - right, just, and fair for the majority of key stakeholders?
    - consistent with his ideals for behaviour, the behaviour others have a right to expect of him, and his sense of duty (deontological test)?
    - producing the best outcome for the greatest number, or the worse outcome for the fewest number (teleological test)?

Given this background (that could appear in an Appendix), we can formulate a recommended course of action for Martin Black to consider. The development of this response will demonstrate one possible approach to this type of case analysis.

Now, developing a response to this case....

Smith's Electric Motorcycles Inc. (SEM)

A recommended course of action for Martin Black.

Introduction (Précis)

Smith's Electronic Motorcycles Inc. (SEM) has been in business since 1995. SEM has produced electric motorcycles branded the Electric Cruiser since 2010 and is developing a better performing version, the Electric Jet, that will be based on the former's platform, using the same battery pack mounting design but augmented two additional rubber grommets. In reviewing design specifications for the Electric Jet and the Electric Cruiser, together with some accident reports, Martin Black, a new member of SEM recently hired as Director of Marketing and Customer Relations, has identified a safety flaw in the form of rubber grommet fatigue, emanating from the rubber grommets. The rubber grommets are sourced from an offshore company. Smith has raised his findings and concerns with Chief Engineer Michael Martin, calling for a design change on the Electric Jet and a recall of all Electric Cruisers, who has advised him to let it go as, based on the information provided by Black, this is a minor matter that could have serious financial consequences for the company. No assumptions have been made in the case analysis that follows.

Author's Note: The introduction portrays the most salient aspects of the case study and sets the stage for the response. It is necessary to anchor your response to the case requirements.

The Primary Problem

Martin Black has discovered that SEM has sold, and plans to sell, a product with potential defects that could harm people and must decide, in the absence of support from the design team, whether to raise this matter directly with the CEO and the Board of Directors.

Author's Note: *As stated the primary problem is clear, and is not a symptom, a cause, or a result of the problem.*

A Secondary Problem

The rubber mounting grommets, the source of the product failure, are procured from an offshore company.

Author's Note: *This is a secondary problem since it is both a symptom and a cause of the primary problem.*

Analysis

A number of key factors will influence the course of action recommended for Martin Black. These will include stakeholders, money, globalization, and ethics.

Author's Note: *other factors may be at play.*

Stakeholders

Key stakeholders for SEM are defined as those persons or organizations with significant power to influence the company and high interest in the activities of the company. This analysis will focus on stakeholders' stakes as related to the primary problem, and is presented in the following table:

Stakeholder	Stake	Relationship to the Primary Problem
Shareholders of SEM	Profit maximization; Return on investment	Investment and return could be adversely affected by both the costs of redesign and recall, or failure of SEM to act on Black's information if problems arose and the information was made public
SEM Board of Directors	A fiduciary duty to act in the best interests of the corporation	Failure to direct the corporation to undertake action to remedy the situation could result in board members being held personally liable for certain outcomes
Customers	Expectation that the product they are purchasing is safe	Customers could be directly affected by SEM's failure to act on the safety risks
Employees	Continuation of SEM as a going concern in order to preserve their employment and livelihood	Redesign and recall costs may be unaffordable by SEM and shutting down might be a cheaper alternative to dealing with the problem
Competition	Market share and competitive advantage	If Black's findings became public, the competition would seize the opportunity to flaunt the safer virtues of their substitute product

Author's Note: Recall from page 9: "…a picture might be worth a thousand words…but is not a substitute for a well-written, thoughtful explanation." The same applies to a table—provided the table is appropriately introduced and contains information that is fully explained, I am personally comfortable with accepting analyses in tabular form, periodically…

A further stakeholder, although not considered "key" would be environmentalists. It is reasonable to expect environmentalists to support and applaud the product and initiative of SEM. It is also reasonable to expect some form of backlash if the environmentalists perceive they were misled and their support for a company that was producing unsafe products was misplaced, however "green" they might be. Depending on the outcome the environmentalists could publicly oppose the company which would have dire consequences given the strength of social media. While the environmentalists could be currently characterised as having high power and low interest, any change in interest level could transform this group into that of a key stakeholder.

Money

SEM is a "for profit" company whose shareholders expect to obtain a return on their investment commensurate with the level of perceived risk associated with the investment instrument. Further, many investors purchase shares in companies that are promoting green technologies and products that are environmentally friendly, for which these investors will often pay a premium.

The SEM investors would be expected to react negatively to knowledge concerning a product design defect that has the potential to cause harm. This reaction could manifest in them selling their shares and investing elsewhere, the result of which could be difficult in SEM obtaining share capital investment going forward, or the shareholder's voting in a new board of directors; either or both of which would have a detrimental effect on the public's perception of SEM and its products. A declining share value and declining sales could ultimately result in the failure of SEM.

Globalization

The rubber grommets are sourced from an offshore company. This may be done for a variety of reasons including cost-savings, specialized raw material sources, or the absence of a domestic manufacturing facility. Regardless of why the grommets are sourced offshore, the responsibility and accountability for quality control rests with SEM. The company should have in place a regular schedule of ways and means to ensure quality on a continuous basis, and to perform regular tests on the product to ensure the integrity of the engineering. In addressing the primary problem, having records to prove quality assurance tests would be a significant help. In their absence, having a plan in place to make this happen would assist in demonstrating concern for the quality of outsourced components in the interests of protecting customers and the general public.

Ethics

The rules and principles that define right and wrong behaviour manifest at many levels: the individual and the organization for example. In this case, Martin Black is confronted with a situation in which, apparently, his personal ethics may not be aligned with those of his employer. Black must decide whether to raise his findings and concerns with the CEO and the Board of Directors.

In contemplating this matter, Black must consider the following:

- How correct and reliable are your findings?
- Is it ethical to "do nothing"?
- Is the decision to raise the matter with the CEO and Board of Directors:
  - Right, just, and fair for the majority of key stakeholders?
  - Consistent with your ideals for behaviour, the behaviour others have a right to expect from him, and your sense of duty?
  - Producing the best outcome for the greatest number, or the worse outcome for the fewest number?

The course of action recommended will therefore need to consider the action's impact on key stakeholders and their possible reaction, the financial impact on SEM, the fact that the root cause of the safety threat is the rubber grommets that are sourced offshore, and the ethics involved.

Restrictions/Constraints

Any course of action must also consider any restrictions or constraints manifest in the information provided in the case. Recognizing that any recommendation is only as good as the information provided that serves as the basis from which to make the recommendation it should be noted that the case does not specifically identify to whom Black reports. Furthermore, the case does not explicitly identify SEM as a publicly held corporation and this has implications on the obligations of the Board of Directors as well as shareholders.

Alternative Courses of Action

On the basis of the analysis, there are two possible courses of action: (1) do nothing immediately; (2) immediately inform the CEO and Board of Directors of the findings.

1. Do Nothing Immediately

The first course of action is to do nothing immediately. This could be based on the observation that the sample size for the accident reports is too small and therefore not statistically valid. Further analyses would be necessary and these would include a larger accident sample size, a validation of the quality control mechanisms to ensure the engineering integrity of the rubber grommets, in-house tests on the effect of temperature change on the rubber grommets physical integrity.

This course of action would have no immediately tangible effects on any of the key stakeholders, although it could be construed as withholding information that might affect the company—provided the data are conclusive. This alternative, at least temporarily, removes the "money" concerns and addresses the matter of the offshore-sourced rubber grommets. The challenge in this alternative falls in the realm of "ethics": It could be argued that doing nothing immediately could be perceived as right, just, and fair for the majority of key stakeholders, and produces the best outcome for the greatest number. Whether this is consistent with Black's ideals for his behavior is a matter that only he can determine. For some, this decision would be ethical; for others, it would not.

2. Immediately Inform the CEO and the Board of Directors of the Findings

This alternative prescribes advising the Chief Executive and the Board of the findings immediately, but in a careful, reasoned fashion.

First, something must be done immediately any delay could reasonably be expected to provide a window for a serious accident to occur, regardless of how remote the chance of occurrence might be.

The report provided to the Chief Executive and the Board should set out the findings in a clear way, indicating the number of accidents reviewed and how representative this sample is. The report should also include recommendations to validate the quality control mechanisms of the offshore supplier to ensure the engineering integrity of the rubber grommets, and to perform in-house tests on the effect of temperature change on the rubber grommets' physical integrity. The report should also recommend retaining a communications specialist (if one does not exist on staff) to develop communications and communication protocols while this internal research is ongoing, if it leaks, and when it is released.

This approach recognizes the sensitivity of the matter as well as the potential impact on key stakeholders. It also provides a margin for determining the depth of the safety problem. This approach is also "ethically consistent"—Black has found a potential safety issue and has raised it to the senior organizational levels. This action is right, just, and fair for the majority of key stakeholders and produces the best outcome for the greatest number. It would be consistent, presumably, with Black's ideals for behaviour.

Before sending the report "upstairs" it is recommended that Black sit with Martin and explain his approach and attempt to have Martin become part of the solution.

Of the two suggested alternatives, this second alternative is recommended.

Author's Note: *Other alternatives may be possible and certainly accepted if logical and fully developed. Readers will note how the alternatives are anchored in the analysis.*

Implementation

The implementation of the recommended course of action would be for Black, with or without Martin, to construct a written report containing the information described above, and request a meeting with the CEO, who would ultimately have the responsibility to inform the Board of Directors, if s/he perceived the matter to be of a strategic nature in the realm of governance—the territory of a board of directors. In no circumstance would this report be relayed as an email attachment!

Author's Note: The detail associated with the implementation plan depends upon the requirement of the case study—the role you are being asked to play, for example. Some instructors would prefer to see the entire content of the implementation play developed—in this case, the actual written report that would be sent to the Chief Executive. This is up to the individual instructor who would make these expectations explicit.

From the approach taken to the case study above, some generalizations can be "extracted" to serve as a "roadmap" for students in dealing with cases of this style. This is presented below.

Approaching Style 2 Case Studies—A Suggested Outline

Component	Guiding Principles
Case Introduction/ Précis	This is a brief synopsis of the case—but not an "executive summary" of the case response. The objective is that the reader will be able to quickly understand what is going on in the case, without having to read the entire case. **This is a difficult component** that is best written after the analysis has been completed because at this point you will have gone through the details so many times that the most important content will be very obvious!
Identify the Primary Problem	This is a critical component that you must get right! A *primary problem* is not a symptom, cause, or a result of the problem. If you remove the primary problem, essentially the "case goes away"
Identify Any Secondary Problems	Secondary problems typically are symptoms, causes, or the result of the primary problem

Component	Guiding Principles
Analysis	This section is all about which factors you feel could be in play that have an impact (directly or indirectly) on the information that is contained in the case study. While there are several, the following are frequently found as having an impact on all organizations—the relevance of these factors will vary, depending on the case: • Impact on people • Impact on stakeholders • Financial impact • Social responsibility Impact • Ethical impact In cases where you are asked to look into the future of an organization as regard competition, for example, this is also the section in which you would perform a SWOT analysis: • Strengths and Weaknesses (Internal to the organization) • Opportunities and Threats (External to the organization)
Restrictions/ Constraints	Restrictions or constraints can take a variety of forms, and generally have an effect on the recommended course of action. In the first instance, they could refer to specific details of the case that are not provided which, if known, could have an impact on the recommended course of action—in this manner, they replace the need to identify "assumptions" in a one-off manner. Although in this context, the restrictions and constraints could certainly be construed as assumptions, they are positioned in such a way as to be explained directly in alignment with the recommended course of action—an approach far more compelling. There are other restraints and conditions that could arrive that are not assumptions, but rather realities of the case study. For example, the impact of a period of high inflation may constrain a government's ability to implement a particular policy; a period of rising interest rates may constrain a corporation's ability to borrow

Component	Guiding Principles
Alternative Courses of Action	What "action options" are available to address the primary problem? What are the timelines (short, medium, long)? What is the best alternative, and why? How will your preferred alternative be more effective than any other alternatives in resolving the primary problem? The alternatives must be realistic and your preferred alternative must be very compelling, fully developed, and fully supported.
Implementation	How will you actually implement your preferred alternative? I particularly like this section of any case because it brings a very real focus to what you are recommending! Many "recommendations" are fabulous outpourings but do not take into account the impact on all areas affected. If money is no deterrent, fully trained staff are in abundance, all key stakeholders are cooperative and supportive—what a utopian scenario! And how unrealistic! In preparing your implementation plan you must be realistic. Timelines for implementation are also critical.

Toward a Grading Rubric

As with the earlier style of case study, it is instructive to provide possible examples of grading rubrics. The starting point would be as previously indicated defining what Exceeds, Fully Meets, Meets Most, and Does Not Meet expectations:

Category	Explanation
Does Not Meet Expectations	There are a number of key concepts missing or given minimal/marginal treatment
Meets Most Expectations	The key concepts are covered, although not in appropriate depth
Fully Meets Expectations	The key concepts are covered in appropriate depth
Exceeds Expectations	The key concepts are thoroughly covered to a level that demonstrates "going above and beyond" to include, for example, a (secondary) research effort that links theoretical constructs directly to the case, presenting a particularly compelling position on the matter at hand

In this particular style of case analysis, each component lends itself to specific content to be evaluated. Each component can be weighed appropriately in assigning the grades, at the discretion of the instructor. With this approach, expectations would be articulated for each component, with a final component added regarding the overall quality and calibre of the written report, noting that instructors may be more specific in the required contents of each section:

- Introduction/Précis
- Primary Problem
- Secondary Problem(s) if Applicable
- Analysis
- Restrictions/Constraints
- Alternative Courses of Action
- Implementation
- Overall Calibre of the Written Report

A possibly guiding rubric for SEM is presented on the following pages.

Associated General Guiding Rubric—SEM

Parameter	Exceeds Expectations A+	Fully Meets Expectations A, A−, B+, B	Meets Most Expectations C+, C, D+, D	Does Not Meet Expectations F
Introduction/ Précis	The introduction is exceptionally well written and perfectly summarizes the case. The primary problem is made extremely clear as is the role the case writer is assuming	The introduction is well written and effectively summarizes the case. The primary problem is clear as is the role the case writer is assuming. The response, while fully meeting expectations, lacks the fine detail necessary to exceed expectations	The introduction is reasonably well written. The primary problem is reasonably clear; the role the case writer is assuming is generally discernable but could be made more clear	There is no introduction OR the introduction is sparse AND/OR does not adequately summarize the case AND/OR does not articulate the primary problem AND/OR the role the case writer is assuming
The Primary Problem	The primary problem is very clear and precise, exceptionally well explained, and the reader clearly understands that this problem is not a symptom, cause, or a result of another important problem	The primary problem is very clear and precise, well explained, and the reader understands that this problem is not a symptom, cause, or a result of another important problem. The response, while fully meeting expectations, lacks the fine detail necessary to exceed expectations	The primary problem is correctly identified and reasonably well explained. In some instances the reader may be left with the impression that the way in which the primary problem is written could suggest it is a symptom, cause, or a result of another important problem	The primary problem is not provided OR the problem provided is NOT the primary problem AND/OR not explained OR not adequately explained

Associated General Guiding Rubric—SEM (continued)

Parameter	Exceeds Expectations A+	Fully Meets Expectations A, A–, B+, B	Meets Most Expectations C+, C, C, D+, D	Does Not Meet Expecta- tions F
Secondary Problems	Secondary problems are extremely clear and exceptionally well described as symptoms, causes, or resulting from the primary problem	Secondary problems are clear and well described as symptoms, causes, or resulting from the primary problem	Secondary problems are reasonably clear described as symptoms, causes, or resulting from the primary problem. In some instances, the reader may be left with the impression that the way in which the secondary problems are written could cloud their clarity as secondary problems within the meaning of "secondary problems"	Secondary problems are NOT provided OR those provided are not secondary problems

Associated General Guiding Rubric—SEM   (continued)

Parameter	Exceeds Expectations A+	Fully Meets Expectations A, A−, B+, B	Meets Most Expectations C+, C, D+, D	Does Not Meet Expectations F
Analysis	The analysis is exceptionally well done—it captures the key factors and discusses each factor with a rigour that reflects effort to use several external documents in researching the factor itself, followed by a very precise application of the information to the case study parameters. For every factor, the reader clearly understands its application to the case study. Nothing is missing.	The analysis is well done, and captures the key factors with reasonable precision. The analysis is supported by a very good level of secondary research and the application of the analysis content to the case is well done. For most factors, the reader understands its application to the case study	The analysis is reasonably well done, and captures most of the key factors. The analysis is supported by an acceptable level of secondary research, although not as broad as responses fully meeting expectations, and the application of the analysis content to the case is acceptable. For most factors, the reader understands its application to the case study, but in some cases it is not clear	There is no analysis OR the analysis is incomplete and poorly developed

Associated General Guiding Rubric—SEM (continued)

Parameter	Exceeds Expectations A+	Fully Meets Expectations A, A–, B+, B	Meets Most Expectations C+, C, D+, D	Does Not Meet Expectations F
Restrictions/ Constraints	The restrictions and constraints are very compelling and perfectly aligned with the suggested alternatives and the recommended alternative	The restrictions and constraints are reasonably compelling and aligned with the suggested alternatives and the recommended alternative	The restrictions and constraints are, for the most part, compelling and aligned with the suggested alternatives and the recommended alternative	There are no restrictions/ constraints, OR they are illogical and not compelling, AND/OR very poorly developed OR not developed
Alternative Course of Action	The alternatives are all realistic and exceptionally well explained and compelling. There are no feasible alternatives not mentioned. The preferred alternative is excellent with logical and compelling timelines	The alternatives are realistic and reasonably well explained and compelling. The preferred alternative is well explained with logical and compelling timelines	The alternatives are realistic and appropriately explained, although further discussion would help clarify certain alternatives. The preferred alternative is palatable, and while there is some reference to timelines, this needs to be more fully explained and developed	There are no alternative courses of action OR those provided are illogical and poorly developed

Associated General Guiding Rubric—SEM *(continued)*

Parameter	Exceeds Expectations A+	Fully Meets Expectations A, A−, B+, B	Meets Most Expectations C+, C, D+, D	Does Not Meet Expectations F
Implementation	The implementation plan is exceptionally well described and matches perfectly with the restrictions/constraints indicated in an earlier section	The implementation plan is well described and matches reasonably well with the restrictions/constraints indicated in an earlier section	The implementation plan is described and for the most part, aligns with the restrictions/constraints indicated in an earlier section	There is no implementation plan OR the plan is poorly described AND/OR illogical and not compelling AND/OR will not address the primary problem
	Particular attention is given to the timelines for implementation and these timelines are well explained	Attention is given to the timelines for implementation and the timelines are reasonably well explained	Some attention is given to the timelines for implementation but the explanation for the timelines could be more fully explained	
	There is little doubt on the part of the reader that the preferred alternative is the correct alternative and will be effective in addressing the primary problem	The reader is persuaded that the preferred alternative is correct and will address the primary problem	The reader is persuaded that the preferred alternative is likely correct and will likely address the primary problem	

Associated General Guiding Rubric—SEM *(continued)*

Parameter	Exceeds Expectations A+	Fully Meets Expectations A, A−, B+, B	Meets Most Expectations C+, C, D+, D	Does Not Meet Expectations F
Overall Calibre of the Written Report	The response is completely free of spelling and grammatical errors The response is exceptionally well written and organized, demonstrating considerable effort and attention to quality Citations are used appropriately	The response is for the most part free of spelling and grammatical errors The response is reasonably well written and organized, demonstrating effort and attention to quality Citations are used appropriately	The response contains spelling and grammatical errors that reflect insufficient attention to detail in proofreading The response is not particularly well written although it is possible to follow the argument in most cases Citations are used appropriately, with minor formatting issues noted.	The response is fraught with grammatical and spelling errors, is poorly written, poorly organized, and demonstrates neither effort nor attention to quality

A Case to Explore...

Hinchy's Outdoor Clothes Inc.

Hinchy's Outdoor Clothes Inc. (HOC) was a small but aggressive manufacturer of outdoor clothes designed for extreme weather conditions. Its product line had been successful internationally, particularly in extreme Northern and Southern geographic regions that experienced the most severe of cold weather conditions. HOC clothes were highly regarded because of superior design, toughness, reliability, and overall exceptional quality. The clothes were effective in protecting against both extreme cold and extreme heat owing to their unique design and material content.

Approaching its third year of operations, HOC was experiencing falling sales and shareholders were becoming nervous about the long-term viability of the company. At a recent shareholders' meeting, the two majority shareholders who collectively controlled the company, suggested to Dan Palmer, the CEO, and the senior management team that HOC needs to make greater effort in marketing its products to warm climates to keep the company financially viable.

While waiting for a flight one afternoon at London's Heathrow Airport, Palmer struck up a conversation with a distinguished-looking individual, Dr. Anthony Clifford who, among other things, had extensive business holdings in Central America and would be interested in procuring a substantial order of military fatigue-coloured pants, jackets, and hats. More specifically he would order 5,000 complete outfits if the price could be set by HOC at US$850 per outfit. As it happened, Palmer and Clifford were on the same flight to New York City and spent the time discussing the potential business arrangement.

For Palmer, this was unbelievable news! Clifford did not require any modifications to the design of the suits Palmer was already producing and it would be a simple matter to source the military fatigue-coloured material with only a minor cost increase. This order would generate a much-needed US$4,250,000 with a profit margin on the sale of around US$1.4 million!

On return, Palmer had a credit check done on Clifford and Palmer's banker reported that Clifford owned several companies that were legitimate and financially sound. Three weeks later, Palmer signed an agreement with Clifford to supply the suits and work on the order would start in three months, during which Palmer would need to retain additional staff to meet the manufacturing schedule.

Several weeks later Palmer held a company party to celebrate his good fortune and in typical style invited several stakeholders, including representatives from civil society, local government, and local suppliers. During the course of the evening Palmer was approached by Willard Smith, a known social activist who publicly criticized private military regimes around the world.

When Smith heard the name "Dr. Clifford" he simply stared at Palmer: "You clearly don't know of this guy, do you Dan," asked Smith. "If you did, I know you would not have, under any circumstances, made this deal! "Dr. Clifford" operates a number of companies throughout the world and many of his "customers" are somewhat less than legitimate, to put it mildly. He is notorious in certain circles as being the "go to" person when certain supplies are needed that otherwise would not be obtainable by the customer. "Dr. Clifford," also known as Juan Guzmanala, procures supplies for at least two brutal foreign military regimes, known for their dictatorial approaches to enforcing whatever law pays the most. You need to distance yourself from this Dan!"

Continued

While Dan was reeling from this information, he contemplated what he should do. An old friend of his was a lobbyist and a well-connected spin-doctor. Dan decided to call him to get some advice on how to move forward.

Required

You are the spin-doctor. Advise Dan.

The Art of Using Case Studies on Examinations

The use of case studies on examinations has in my experience, taken three predominant forms: (1) one massive case that is, in fact, the examination; (2) a relatively substantial case that forms a significant percentage of the examination grade, supplemented by short-answer style questions and/or multiple-choice questions; and (3) a series of vignettes or smaller cases (or related popular press articles) embedded in a mainstream examination that test the application of specific concepts.

The good news is that the use of case studies as an examining tool is an excellent approach to test the ability of students to apply theoretical concepts; the bad news is that to do so effectively is difficult and takes considerable time.

There are two important perspectives from which to consider this subject: the instructor and the student.

From the instructor's perspective, there are certain realities:

- Finding or writing a case study that is appropriately tailored to the course material;
- Using a case study that is of sufficient depth to actually test the concepts within the time constraints governed by the examination;
- Setting and communicating the expectations on responses, given the first two bullets, and recognizing that you may have not used cases during the semester, or you may have used a case study as a major deliverable that creates the expectation of an appropriate response in the minds of your students;
- Building in the appropriate additional examination time required to read and understand the cases, and to respond to the requirements;
- Keeping the requirements simple without compromising the integrity of the testing instrument.

From the student's perspective, there are certain realities:

- Cases used on examinations do not lend themselves to what I refer to as "responses by rote." For example, an examination question on leadership might ask you to "define supportive leadership," whereas a case on leadership might ask that you "discuss the style of leadership best exemplified" by whatever is going on in the case—which may or may not be obvious at first glance!
- You will need to carefully budget your time!
- You will need to adjust your headset in terms of requirements: on an exam you are not writing a formal case report—you are answering the questions.

- You will be operating under a time constraint and will be feeling pressured—this is, of course, part of the game—don't become unhinged when you encounter the case(s) on the exam—recognize it for what it is and pay close attention to the marks it (they) represent as this will give you an approximate indication of the time expected to be spent on the response.

The examples that follow are intended to serve two purposes: to provide instructors with ideas through which to catalyze their own innovative ideas, and to provide students with examples that provide ideas on the type of examination case-driven questions they could be expected to encounter.

As an example of **a case study representing "Form 2 – a relatively substantial case" above**, that I have used in the past on an examination, consider the following for which an outline of acceptable responses (Grading Guidance) are provided for illustration only. This case represented 50 percent of the marks possible on the final examination (of three hours duration).

The University College of Management of South March [14]

The University College of Management of South March (UCMSM) was founded in 2008 by five wealthy philanthropists. Two were from East Asia, one was from the United Kingdom, the fourth was from Canada, and the final founder was from Japan. All were highly successful businessmen and well educated, each holding a postgraduate degree in business administration.

---

[14] Case written by Dr. David H. J. Delcorde, Telfer School of Management, University of Ottawa, 2011. This case is fictitious. Any similarities to persons or organizations is purely coincidental.

The UCMSM was intended to be a small but elite institution, whose graduates would be very well received by industry and government. Offering only graduate degree programs in business administration and international business, it was a private school "of deep pockets" as the academic community referred to it, but no one could argue that the calibre of its graduates was stellar and world-class.

Entirely funded by the philanthropist founders and their vast network of successful and influential international business contacts (who contributed very significant amounts of money to UCMSM every year), it received no government funding—nor did it want any government support. The UCMSM benefited from the best of equipment, small class sizes, well-qualified professors with industry and government experience who were paid at least 40 percent more than their equivalents in publicly funded universities, and an ongoing inflow of guest speakers—leaders in industry and government from around the world.

The university did not have any unions. The ten professors were all tenured; five were full professors, and five were associate professors. The full professors were paid $285,000 per year; the associate professors were paid $190,000 per year. Each professor received a rich benefit package including:

- Full medical and dental coverage;
- Paid sick leave amounting to 1.5 days per month, that could accumulate without an upper limit;
- July and August off for vacation, fully paid;
- Two weeks off for vacation over Christmas;
- Living accommodation in campus-owned executive suites paid by the university college;

- Parking paid by the university college;
- Paid travel expenses whenever they travelled to present research papers.

The professors were also the beneficiaries of an incentive award system through which they were encouraged to research and publish. Through the award system they would receive a paid bonus for every research paper published in a list of top-tier academic journals:

- For no publishing, no bonus (and academic probation imposed);
- For publishing up to five articles in a given year, a bonus of 10 percent of the professor's gross salary;
- For publishing between five and ten articles in a given year, a bonus of 15 percent of the professor's gross salary;
- For publishing more than ten articles in a given year, a bonus of 20 percent of the professor's gross salary.

In addition to being required to publish at least one academic research paper per year, every professor was required to maintain a student performance rating average of not less than four out of five on certain key questions in the assessment questionnaire prepared by all students for each professor at the end of the course. The questions dealt with the students' perception of the professor as a teacher, his or her ability to teach, his or her level of preparation, and his/her ability to engage the students and make the subject matter interesting.

Many major corporations recruited their executive cadre from the UCMSM; many more corporations sent their executives to the UCMSM for graduate degrees. As well, governments from around the world sent their senior executives to the UCMSM for postgraduate work as well as to network and better understand government-business relations. It was tough to get in, and tough to succeed, but once accepted a graduate was guaranteed a well-paying job—many students had high-paying job offers even before graduation (assuming they graduated!).

While research was extremely important to the UCMSM and indeed its professors undertook leading edge research in many important areas, its focus was on high-quality teaching and learning, and developing tangible skills that could be put to practical use immediately upon graduation.

The UCMSM offered only two degrees: a general MBA and a Master of Arts in International Business Management (MAIBM). While course-intensive, both programs required an empirically based research paper as a component of the curriculum. No part-time programs were offered, and students remained on campus for the duration of their twelve-month program. Courses were not offered during the summer months, as this was time reserved to conduct research.

Under the direction of the university President (officially referred to as the *Principle and Chancellor*), Dr. Jethro Smith, the UCMSM's ten professors were drawn from a range of cultures and the university enrolled no more than one hundred students per year in each program. This roughly translated into class sizes of no more than ten students per class. There were waiting lists to get in and demand was growing. After considerable deliberations, the founders agreed that in order to meet the demand for its services it would be necessary to increase the number of students. This had everything to do with demand, and absolutely nothing to do with the need for revenues from tuition—the UCMSM *didn't need the money from tuition*—in fact tuition was only $2,500 per year: a token amount collected to meet legislative requirements—that was subsequently donated to charity. Even living expenses for the students while registered at the university were covered.

In reflecting on the need to enroll more students it became obvious to Smith that much of the university's success was a result of its learning culture and bureaucratic simplicity—the professors and Smith were a tight group and shared similar philosophies and favoured simple administrative guidelines and regulations. With the impending increase in students, it would be necessary to augment the staff and by Smith's estimates, an additional two professors would be required. While many professors would be attracted to the UCMSM environment, its quality of life, and rich salaries and benefits, only a certain type of professors would be retained. Smith sketched out the following attributes of the "perfect" candidate:

- An earned doctorate degree;
- An established research program in a leading edge area;
- Teaching experience with consistently high ratings;
- Experience in supervising graduate students undertaking research projects;
- Cross-cultural management experience;
- At least ten years of full-time successful senior management experience in either the private, public, or volunteer sector;
- A conscientious extravert, curious, imaginative, willing to entertain new ideas, good natured, trusting, and helpful.

He also expected his professors to teach full loads of five courses per year, and since this demanded standing in front of classes for extended periods of time, any candidate with a disability that precluded this would be disqualified. As well, because of the reputation of the university and the need to project an active and engaged ambiance, he did not intend to entertain the candidature of anyone who was seriously overweight or out of shape as he thought this would reflect poorly on the institution.

It was Smith's view that the best approach to this might be to retain an independent but highly experienced consultant to take care of the recruitment activities necessary and participate with Smith and the other founders in interviewing the candidates.

Annex A

The following candidates have been short-listed and will be interviewed for the two positions of professor at the UCMSM. All candidates have prior teaching experience, are involved in leading-edge research projects, and have supervised graduate students.

Maxime Artois

Nationality: French (born in Paris, February 24th, 1952)

Academic Credentials: MBA (Stanford), Doctor of Philosophy (software engineering) (MIT)

Recent Experience: 2000 to present: CEO of a major French software developer in Paris; 1995 to 2000 entrepreneur—established his own successful software company in Belgium that was bought out by the French company where he currently serves as CEO.

Big 5 Profile:

	Upper Quartile	Median	Lower Quartile
Conscientiousness		X	
Agreeableness	X		
Neuroticism		X	
Openness to Experience			X
Extraversion	X		

Walther Krueger

Nationality: German (born in Munich, April 15th, 1955)

Academic Credentials: Master of Mechanical Engineering (MIT), MBA (University of Ottawa), Doctor of Philosophy (Management) (State University of New York), Doctor of Business Administration (The Open University, UK).

Recent Experience: 2006 to present: Vice President of Operations, Porsche AG (Germany); 2000 to 2006: Vice President Bombardier (Montreal); 1995 to 2000: Senior Human Resources Manager, Canadian National Railway (Toronto).

Big 5 Profile:

	Upper Quartile	Median	Lower Quartile
Conscientiousness	X		
Agreeableness		X	
Neuroticism		X	
Openness to Experience			X
Extraversion	X		

Susan Takaheto

Nationality: Japanese (born in Tokyo, July 12th, 1965)

Academic Credentials: Master of Chemical Engineering (Harvard), MBA (Carleton), Master of Electrical Engineering (Waterloo), Doctor of Philosophy (Business Administration) (Cambridge, UK).

Recent Experience: 2005 to present: Associate Vice President, British Telecom (London, UK); 1999 to 2005: Vice President Engineering, Union Carbide, India; 1995 to 1999: Senior Director, Japanese Engineering Research Institute, Nagasaki.

Big 5 Profile:

	Upper Quartile	Median	Lower Quartile
Conscientiousness	X		
Agreeableness		X	
Neuroticism			X
Openness to Experience	X		
Extraversion	X		

Required

You are the consultant retained by Smith. Referring as necessary to the profiles of each of the three candidates short-listed in Annex A, please respond to each of the following questions:

1. Define *organizational citizenship behaviour* (OCB) (4 marks) and briefly discuss which aspects of the attributes of Smith's idea of the perfect candidate would constitute OCB (4 marks).

Grading Guidance:

Organizational citizenship behaviour, also referred to as extra-role behaviour, describes behaviour which goes above and beyond expected behaviour. Such behaviours include persisting with enthusiasm and extra effort, helping and cooperating with others, endorsing and defending organizational objectives (4 marks)

The attributes of Smith's idea of the perfect candidate that would demonstrate organizational citizenship behaviours might include (4 marks):

- *Conscientiousness*
- *Imaginative*
- *Good natured*
- *Trusting*
- *helpful*

2. Using Hofstede's four dimensions (ignore long-term orientation) of national culture develop cultural profiles for each of the three candidates short-listed in Annex A (2 marks for each profile). Be certain to describe each dimension (2 marks each). You may wish to use a chart but this is not necessary. Which cultural profile do you feel would be best suited to the organizational climate at UCMSM as portrayed in the case (2 marks)?

Grading Guidance:
The cultural profiles of the applicants were covered in class under a different scenario.

Dimension	Maxime Artois French (2 marks)	Walther Krueger German (2 marks)	Susan Takaheto Japanese (2 marks)
Power Distance	High	Low	High
Uncertainty Avoidance	High	High	High
Individualism	High	High	Low
Masculinity-Femininity	Feminine	Masculine	Masculine

Definitions of the Dimensions

Power Distance (2 marks)—how a society deals with the fact that people are unequal is a social and status sense: high power distance cultures accept the unequal sharing of power.

Uncertainty Avoidance (2 marks)—how society copes with uncertainty and deals with risk: High uncertainty avoidance cultures are uncomfortable deviating from the norm, does not like uncertainty and are risk averse.

Individualism (2 marks)—the relative closeness of the relationship between one person and others: low-individualism cultures are collectivist with emphasis on groups.

Masculinity-Femininity (2 marks)—the sexuality of roles in society and the degree to which society allows overlap between the roles of men and women: A masculine society is aggressive, competitive, with gender-specific roles.

The organizational climate at UCMSM might suggest a cultural profile that embeds equality, risk-taking, balanced individualism, and a less masculine orientation. While none of the candidates line up perfectly, Krueger might be the best fit (I am certainly open to other suggestions with the appropriate justification) (2 marks).

3. Develop two questions that you would ask the people provided as references by each candidate (2 marks each).

Grading Guidance:
I am looking for questions that would extract concrete examples from the referee that are linked to Smith's attributes of an ideal candidate. For example, "Tell me about a time when Mr. Krueger entertained a new idea that was to some extent counter to his own views and practices." How did he handle this? What was the outcome? (2 marks for each question to a maximum of 4 marks)

4. Job satisfaction is generally determined by perceptions of organizational justice. Define distributive, procedural, and interactional justice (2 marks each). In your view, the absence of which one of these would most adversely affect each of the candidates and why (2 marks for the analysis of each candidate)? In supporting your position you will need to reference each candidate's "Big Five" profile appearing in the attached Annex as well as their Hofstede cultural profiles you derived in an earlier question.

Grading Guidance:
Distributive justice refers to the appropriateness of outcomes—rewarding employees based on their contributions, proving each employee with roughly the same compensation, providing a benefit based on one personal requirement (2 marks).

Procedural justice refers to the perceived fairness of the decision-making process used to distribute rewards (2 marks).

Interactional justice refers to the perception of the fairness of the interpersonal treatment (2 marks).

Responding to the second part of the question requires a consideration of the cultural profiles as well as the Big 5 results.

Artois: accepts unequal sharing of power, prefers not to take risks, and is individualistic but not as aggressive or competitive as Krueger or Takaheto. He is agreeable, extraverted, and not particularly open. He might be most adversely affected by shortcomings in interactional justice (2 marks).

Krueger: prefers equal power sharing, is risk-averse, individualistic, and competitive. He is conscientious, extraverted, and not particularly open. He might be most adversely affected by shortcomings in distributive justice (2 marks).

Takaheto: accepts unequal sharing of power, is risk averse and collectivist, and competitive. She is conscientious, extraverted, and open. She would likely be most adversely affected by shortcomings in procedural justice (2 marks).

5. In your view, is Smith's intention to not entertain the candidature of anyone who is seriously overweight or out of shape legal (4 marks)?

    Grading Guidance:
    To be "legal" this would have to be based on a bona fide occupation requirement (BFOR). BFOR would require that it:

    -   *is a necessary (not merely preferred) requirement for performing a job, and,*
    -   *must be based on sound (and defensible) Job Analysis.*

    It is very unlikely that Smith's intention could be based on a bona fide occupational requirement and a good response would present a reasonably well-developed argument (for or against, but in every case, provide the definition of a BFOR (4 marks).

6. Which two of the candidates would you hire? Support your decision (6 marks).

Grading Guidance:
This question looks for a well-developed response supported by the tools used throughout this examination. A good response would include an analysis that supports a decision based on:

- *Prevailing organizational environment;*
- *The "ideal" candidate as envisioned by Smith, with the appropriate compromises as necessary;*
- *Big 5 profile;*
- *Cultural profile;*
- *Likeliness of organizational citizenship behaviour;*
- *Other information from the case or from the candidates' bios (6 marks).*

Another example of a case study that I have used in the past on an examination, consider the following for which an outline of acceptable responses (Grading Guidance) is provided for illustration only. This question was presented on the examination as a "Scenario" and represented 20 percent of the possible marks available on the final examination.

Canadian Farmers for Fairness

You are a Consultant lobbyist registered with the Government of Canada. A small nonprofit association *"Canadian Farmers for Fairness"* has contacted you through your website. You have agreed to meet with Association representatives at 4:00 PM tomorrow afternoon. The Association is aware that the federal government is considering the development of legislation that would make differentiating between genetically modified foods and nongenetically modified foods unnecessary. The Association would like you to provide them with advice on how to develop a strategy through which to lobby the federal government to make the labelling of genetically modified foods mandatory across Canada.

Required

List the points you would make to the Association to advise them on:

1. Your particular category as a consultant compared with other categories (2 Marks).

2. What their lobbying strategy <u>outline</u> might look like (and what brief recommendations you would offer in each stage of the lobbying strategy—e.g., direct approach vs. quiet diplomacy, etc.). Note: ignore dealing with the costs of this lobbying strategy since you do not have sufficient information to advise them on this. Note also that you are <u>not expected to develop a full lobbying strategy!</u> (12 marks)

3. At what point in the public policy process (more specifically at which steps) would this lobbying effort be most effective (and why), and your view on the effect the amount of money invested in the lobbying effort would have on a positive outcome. (6 marks)

Grading Guidance:

Part 1 (2 Marks):

Consultant Lobbyists are professional third-party paid lobbyists. In house lobbyists are employees who, as a significant part of their duties, lobby on behalf of their employer (associations/not-for-profits or corporations).

Part 2 (12 Marks–2 marks per step as outlined below—1 mark for identifying the step; 1 mark for the recommendation—note the recommendation does not have to be as given below, but must be reasonable and logical):

Lobbying Strategy Outline

- *Must clearly define and frame the issue*
  - *Possible Recommendation: The difference between genetically modified foods and nongenetically modified foods is of a concern to Canadians and there is a need to create or increase the level of awareness.*
- *Must decide whether the issue strategic or operational*
  - *Possible Recommendation: This is a strategic issue because it involves legislation, would likely incorporate public opinion, etc.*
- *Must decide whom you would lobby*
  - *Possible Recommendations: Minister of Agriculture and Agri-foods, the genetically modified foods industry, bureaucrats, major food retailers.*
- *Must decide on which techniques you would use*
  - *Possible Recommendations: a combination of direct and indirect techniques. Direct techniques: meetings with bureaucrats, the minister, major food retailers; Indirect techniques: use of media, advocacy advertising.*
- *Must decide on what type of lobbyist to use*
  - *Possible Recommendation: a consultant lobbyist (because, after all, this is your job) combined with the efforts of an industry association*
- *Must analyze how successful this strategy might (or might not be)*
  - *Possible Recommendation: The association can expect considerable push back from government, the genetically modified food industry, and the major food retailers. The greatest opportunity for success would come from public pressure on elected officials. If the lobby is*

successful, it could have a negative impact on the genetically modified food industry as well as on related research efforts, etc.

Part 3 (6 Marks):

As the government is in the early stages of modifying this legislation, now is the time. The lobby can have the greatest effect in the problem formulation, policy agenda, and to a lesser degree, the policy formulation stages in the public policy process because this is where costs and degree of influence is optimized. **(3 Marks)**

The influence of money would be important in this case as considerable investment would be needed to mount a sufficiently strong and very public advocacy campaign to develop enough political risk to influence politicians. **(3 Marks)**

Two additional examples demonstrate the use of both a case study, and a popular press article in a multiple-choice construct.

The Yellow Velo

Peter Smith recently graduated from the Telfer School of Management with a B.Com in marketing. An "entrepreneur" in spirit, he was keenly interested in starting his own company. One of his passions was cycling and he always believed that regardless of how sophisticated bicycles had become, there was always room for improvement, particularly in their use of both "green" materials and "green suppliers."

In March of 2012, Peter had a chance meeting with Mitchell Marcus Mylo III (better known as "MMM"). MMM was a very successful businessman known to invest in certain start-up companies in exchange for an ownership slice. MMM had been a guest lecturer at Smith's Entrepreneurship course and had left quite an impression. Over coffee and donuts at MMM's coffee café in downtown, Shawinigan Peter tossed some thoughts around with MMM. Several hours later, a plan emerged to develop and sell the *Yellow Velo*. The Company would be called **Smith's Yellow Velo**.

The idea was that MMM would partner with Smith, remaining anonymous to the public but taking an active management role. This was desirable since MMM's business holdings were very diversified and international in scope. He had contacts across the globe with suppliers in a range of industries and the components Smith would need could be easily found by MMM. In terms of the approach to business, Smith would procure component parts and assemble the bicycles in Shawinigan. Given the importance of assembly time and that all assembly would be done by hand, Smith used a PERT chart to set out the assemblies critical path:

Event	Description	Expected Time (Hours)	Preceding Event
A	Inventory all component parts	0.5	None
B	Attach pedals and sprockets to the frame	0.25	A
C	Attach gears and gear-changing components	0.15	B
D	Attach brakes and cables	0.25	B
E	Install tires on wheels and check balance	0.30	C, D
F	Install wheels on the frame	0.15	E
G	Install seat	0.10	F
H	Setup and test	0.25	G
I	Package for shipping and put in inventory	0.20	H

Smith intended only to produce a "green" bicycle (not the colour, but rather an environmentally friendlier bicycle than anything currently produced). He believed that people would pay a premium for this and so did MMM. Of course the costs of producing such a bicycle would be high—and so would the selling price. After an exhaustive search for "green" component suppliers, Smith's costs were as follows:

Component	Cost ($)
Frame	145
Wheel	60
Tire	15
Gear assembly	85
Brake assembly	45
Seat	10
Packaging	30

Smith hired two students to assemble, test, and package the bicycles. Each student was paid $15 per hour. He rented a warehouse from MMM to set up his company. His monthly rent payment to MMM was $335. Utilities (water, hydro, etc.) amounted to $90 per month. Interest on his bank loan to start up the company was $100 per month. To enter the market and get established, MMM counselled Smith on not charging excessively until the Yellow Velo "caught on." Taking MMM's advice, Smith set the selling price at $600 per bicycle.

MMM cautioned Smith that if his Yellow Velo became popular, he could expect challenges from other manufacturers and he should spend some time thinking about what his reaction would be to actions by competitors to enter his market.

As Smith's company grew, he hired more employees for assembly as well as marketing. He also spent more time selling his product and working with his suppliers. His staff now numbered thirty-five persons and his simple organization structure, with everyone reporting directly to him, was no longer effective. He put in place a more formalized structure with managers over three main divisions: administration, manufacturing, and sales and marketing. Smith believed in delegation and soon became known as an enthusiastic, self-confident leader whose personality and actions influence people to behave in certain ways.

Smith's manufacturing process has expanded to the point where he has implemented an "assembly line" approach through which a Yellow Velo moves through stations where specific components are added. For example, one person installs pedals and sprockets to the frame, following which the partially assembled frame moves to a subsequent station where a person installs gears, brakes, and cables. Every person on the assembly line has the authority to stop the process in the event he or she notices something that appears to be incorrect. This system of control helps to ensure a high-quality product.

Smith enjoyed impressive success in his first two years of operations and his partnership with MMM continues to work well.

Questions

1. Which of the following **best** describes MMM's involvement in Smith's Yellow Velo?

    a. General Partner

    b. Limited Partner

    c. Secret Partner

    d. Silent Partner

2. Based on Smith's PERT chart, the critical path to produce one Yellow Velo bicycle would be:

    a. 1 hour

    b. 2 hours

   c. 30 minutes

   d. 1.85 hours

3. Based on the variable and fixed costs, to breakeven every month, Smith would need to sell

   a. 5 bicycles

   b. 10 bicycles

   c. 2.9 bicycles

   d. 3.9 bicycles

4. Based on the variable and fixed costs, for Smith to earn a profit of $31,500 per year, he would need to sell

   a. 15 bicycles per month

   b. 45 bicycles per month

   c. 20 bicycles per month

   d. 30 bicycles per month

5. When MMM cautions Smith to consider what actions he might take in response to actions from his competition, MMM is recommending that Smith undertake:

   a. Scenario planning

   b. Contingency planning

   c. Strategic planning

   d. Operational planning

6. The type of leadership style demonstrated by Smith is

   a. Charismatic

   b. Transformational

   c. Transactional

   d. Visionary

7. The type of departmentalization that best describes Smith's organization is:

   a. Product

   b. Geographic

   c. Functional

   d. Customer

8. The approach to quality control on the assembly line is an example of a

   a. Feedforward control

   b. Feedback control

   c. Concurrent control

   d. Strategic control

9. Given the information in the case concerning Smith's company, which of the following quality standards is most likely not achievable by Smith's Yellow Velo?

   a. ISO 9000

   b. ISO 14001

   c. Six Sigma

   d. ISO 26000

10. If customers consistently complained only about the difficulty in having the Yellow Velo serviced in their local market, this would represent a failure in which product quality dimensions?

    a. Performance

    b. Conformance

    c. Serviceability

    d. Perceived Quality

Articles in the Popular Press— A "Quasi-Vignette"

While not considered a "case study" per se, popular press articles often raise current events that are linked to classroom subject matter. These articles frequently offer the opportunity for students to apply theoretical knowledge to events that are currently happening in the world. While it is possible to use these articles as quasi cases, I have limited their use to examinations, and in the multiple-choice or True/ False format, and the short answer format.

The following provide examples that I have used in the past.

Applying the Multiple-choice or True/ False Format

The following article by Paul Wiseman appeared in the *Globe and Mail* on November 2nd, 2018.[15] Indicate whether the response to each of the three statements following this article is true or false.

---

[15] Wiseman, Paul. "*U.S. Trade Deficit Grows for Fourth Straight Month.*" The Globe and Mail Inc. November 2, 2018, https://www.theglobeandmail.com/business/article-us-trade-deficit-grows-for-fourth-straight-month/, Accessed June 24, 2019.

U.S. Trade Deficit Grows For Fourth Straight Month

PAUL WISEMAN

Washington

The Associated Press

Published November 2, 2018

Record imports expanded the U.S. trade deficit for the fourth straight month in September, as the politically sensitive trade deficit in goods with China hit a record.

The Commerce Department said Friday that the gap between what America sells and what it buys abroad climbed to $54 billion, up 1.3 per cent from $53.3 billion in August and the highest level since February.

Imports climbed 1.5 per cent to a record $266.6 billion, led by an influx of telecommunications equipment and clothing. Exports also rose 1.5 per cent to $212.6 billion, led by increases in shipments of civilian aircraft and petroleum products.

President Donald Trump has made a priority of reducing America's huge, persistent trade deficits. Despite his tariffs on imported steel and aluminum and on Chinese goods, the deficit so far this year is up 10.1 per cent to $445.2 billion. The goods deficit with China rose by 4.3 per cent in September to a record $40.2 billion.

China and other countries have counterpunched with import taxes on American products. U.S. exports of soybeans, targeted for retaliatory tariffs by China, dropped 29.4 per cent in September.

Trump sees the lopsided trade numbers as a sign of U.S. economic weakness and as the result of bad trade deals and abusive practices by U.S. trading partners, especially China.

Mainstream economists view trade deficits as the result of an economic reality unlikely to yield to changes in trade policy: Americans buy more than they produce, and imports fill the gap. The strong U.S. economy also encourages Americans to buy more foreign products.

U.S. exports are also hurt by the American dollar's role as the world's currency. The dollar is usually in high demand because it is used in so many global transactions. That means the dollar is persistently strong, raising prices of U.S. products and putting American companies at a disadvantage in foreign markets.

In September, the United States ran a $23.2 billion surplus in the trade of services such as banking and tourism. But that was offset by a $77.2 billion deficit in the trade of goods such as cellphones and cars.

From "U.S. Trade Gap Grew to $54 Billion in September" by Paul Wiseman November 2, 2018. Copyright © 2018 by The Associated Press. Reprint by permission.

1. If the American dollar were to be devalued in the global currency exchange market, the price of U.S. products would fall giving American companies an advantage in foreign markets...T/F

2. One intention of the imposition of tariffs on Chinese goods was intended to discourage American consumers from buying the Chinese goods in favour of domestic goods...T/F

3. A rise in the interest rate could cause American consumers to spend less; ultimately this could increase the imports demanded by Americans...T/F

Applying the Short Answer Format

The following was published on May 11, 2017.[16] Respond to each of the three questions following this article.

---

[16] PepsiCo Greater ChinaRegion (GCR) signs strategic agreement with online retailer Alibaba", PotatoPRO.com, May 22, 2017, https://www.potatopro.com/news/2017/pepsico-greater-china-region-gcr-signs-strategic-agreement-online-retailer-alibaba, accessed June 24, 2019.

SHANGHAI, May 11, 2017 /PRNewswire/ – PepsiCo Greater China Region (GCR) signed a strategic agreement with Alibaba Group, the world's largest online and mobile commerce company. The collaboration enables PepsiCo to further enhance consumer experiences by leveraging Alibaba's data to introduce innovative marketing initiatives, customized products and integrated omnichannel solutions. The agreement was signed at the PepsiCo Asia R&D Center in Shanghai, by Mike Spanos, PepsiCo GCR President & CEO, and Jet Jing, Vice President of Alibaba Group.

"Developing our e-commerce business is one of PepsiCo's strategic priorities," said Mike Spanos, PepsiCo GCR President & CEO. "Through this collaboration, we will fully take advantage of Alibaba's platform and data to carry out more innovative experiments, perfect PepsiCo's products and services, and enhance online consumer experiences. Our joint effort with Alibaba will help us lead the ever-changing consumer trend and better serve Chinese consumers."

Jet Jing, Vice President of Alibaba Group, added: "We are pleased to collaborate with PepsiCo, a leading multinational company. Alibaba Group is committed to enabling brands by helping them leverage our big data capabilities and omnichannel solutions to further drive strategic growth in the China market."

The strategic agreement is built upon the existing success between PepsiCo and Alibaba in their e-commerce partnership. Since establishing a flagship store on Tmall in 2012, PepsiCo has launched a series of innovative online marketing initiatives. Recent examples include PepsiCo's 2016 Super Brand Day, Quaker's co-branded campaign with Tmall during Alibaba's 11.11 Global Shopping Festival, and Kumamon-branded Lay's gift campaign during Chinese New Year. In addition, PepsiCo expanded its reach in rural China by leveraging the distribution channels through Alibaba's Rural Taobao program.

As one of the leading food & beverage companies in the world, PepsiCo is a global leader in developing and marketing brands. Alibaba Group provides a comprehensive suite of solutions on brand building, channel management and product innovation by tapping into the insights generated from consumer data. The collaboration leads the evolving digital transformation of the food and beverage industry in China.

From "PepsiCo Signs Strategic Agreement with Alibaba Group" May 11, 2017. Copyright © 2017 by PepsiCo. Reprinted by permission.

1. Does the initiative between PepsiCo and Alibaba exemplify a strategic alliance? Support your position.

2. Would any effort by Shanghai to impose performance requirements such as local content or local participation in top management represent policies to restrict Foreign Direct Investment? Support your position.

3. If PepsiCo USA purchased Alibaba, would this represent Foreign Direct Investment? Support your position.

Final Thoughts

This book has presented suggested approaches to preparing business and management style cases studies, focusing on those cases accompanied by direct questions and those cases that are more "open ended" in their requirements.

An example of each style of case has been presented and analyzed, and associated suggested guiding evaluation rubrics have been included, leading to more generalized "playbooks" that students can use to assist in developing responses.

The practice of using case studies on examinations has been considered, with examples provided of cases and responses that have been successfully used in class, including longer cases, short cases, and popular press articles that require "short answer" responses to specific questions or responses to multiple-choice or True/False related questions.

It is important to emphasize that while this book provides a perspective on preparing cases analyses, there are many other views and approaches to *the art of business and management case analysis.*

What follows next is a selection of cases that instructors may wish to consider for use in their classes. These cases have been organized by main subject matter; some containing suggested questions/requirements; others without. Most instructors would prefer to develop their own requirements to any given case study, and these "requirements" would be expected to change semester by semester.

1. General Business/Management Cases

2. Human Resources Cases

3. Marketing Cases

4. Accounting, Finance, and Internal Auditing Cases

5. Cases Involving the Interactions of Business, Government, and Civil Society

Each section is preceded by a brief introduction, followed by a list of the cases included in the section with general subject matter. Unless otherwise noted, all cases have been written by the author (over the past several years). Any resemblance to persons or organizations is purely coincidental.

General Business/ Management Cases

General Business/Management Cases is a somewhat vague nomenclature. This is deliberate and intended to indicate that the cases selected for inclusion do not necessary fit neatly into other specialized areas such as, for example, Human Resources Management, Marketing, Accounting and Finance Cases, and other areas. The cases selected cover a range of areas as indicated below, in order of appearance.

Case Title	General Area of Focus	Page No.
Leadership Behaviours at the Iron Oxide Mineral Corporation	Leadership styles	100
Fairborne Manufacturing Company	Types of partners; corporate raider; mergers and takeovers	105
Downsizing the Apex Corporation (Part 1)	Downsizing options	107
The Apex Corporation (Part 2)— Downsizing: Which Manager Gets Let Go?	Implementing one of two downsizing options and deciding which senior manager must be let go	118
The Kilowatt Electric Car Corporation	Organizational structures—functional, geographic, product line departmentalization	120
Marty's Mall Mart	Organizing a business	122
Water Street Optical	Small business, entrepreneurship, forms of business ownership	125
Governance at the Ronin Utilities of Inner Newfoundland (RUIN) Corporation	Corporate governance	131
Exclusive Limousine Ltd.	Planning	134
Huang Chow Enterprises (HCE)	International business, strategic alliances, government	135
Arthur Cox	Cross-cultural team management	139
Northern Alkaline Battery Recycling Company Ltd.	Ethics and social responsibility	146
Stromboni Race car Corporation	Crisis planning	147
Kevin's Mobile Frozen Yoghurt	Decision-making under uncertainty	148

Leadership Behaviours at the Iron Oxide Mineral Corporation

The Iron Oxide Mineral Corporation (IOMC) was a publicly held Canadian mining company operating in Canada's far north. James Joner Javier (JJJ), a qualified mining engineer, was the Chief Operating Officer and had been with the firm since 1982 as one of its first employees when it started as a penny stock prospecting company. In its thirty-six year plus history, IOMC had progressed from a high-risk, small time, relatively obscure mining company to a highly respected major international player in the mining of diamonds and precious gemstones. Much of the company's success was due to the uncanny and sustaining ability of Javier to locate areas of high yield and to mine the areas at lower cost than most of the competition, as well the very low level of staff turnover at all levels—in the past five years the only staff departures had occurred due to retirements. This allowed IOMC the luxury of not always having to urgently train new' employees and to adopt careful and managed succession plans.

JJJ, occasionally referred to as "J-cubed" by some of his followers, was a highly competent mining engineer with Bachelor and Master degrees in applied science, as well as an MBA degree. JJJ was well respected as a professional engineer—regarded as the best in the business by his peers, and had received many awards over the years relating to innovation in mining. Notwithstanding his exalted status in the company as its Chief Operating Officer, JJJ spent as much time in the field with his sleeves rolled up as he did in the boardroom. Very self-confident, there were no tasks his staff could do that he could not. This was no small accomplishment as all of his staff were competent and highly skilled in a wide variety of tasks ranging from intricate computer modelling and essay analysis to operating heavy equipment.

This knowledge and ability provided JJJ with credibility as a fair assessor of the performance of his followers, who also perceived his assessments as being fair. The nature of the mining industry today demands that accurate performance measures are developed and articulated for the numerous skilled jobs at hand, and that the overall performance of the mine depends, to a great extent, on the skills, efforts, and abilities of the workers. JJJ supported those workers who worked hard, replaced those who did *not* with those who *would* work hard, and was not shy about clearly outlining his expectations, telling the workers the best way to do their jobs and how *not* to do their jobs. In the last thirty-five years JJJ had "replaced" only ten employees for cause—out of an average total staff complement of 205.

JJJ was also known as a manager who ran a "tight" ship, and believed strongly in remuneration directly related to performance. Performance, in his mind, was about both effectiveness but also efficiency. All staff were encouraged to look for ways to cut costs without sacrificing quality, and any staff member or staff group who suggested sensible, practical, and implementable cost-cutting approaches to mining processes were provided with incentive bonuses—cash, time off, first choice of shifts, or some combination thereof. At the same time staff whose work was not up to par, or whose sloppiness resulted in a waste of company resources were docked pay, and given last pick for vacation time and shifts. As well, every employee shared in a certain percentage of company profits when the profits exceeded a predetermined threshold. The profit sharing typically took the form of company shares that could be sold on the stock market, or retained as an investment. Over the last ten years, every employee of IOMC had received an amount of profit share that represented 6 percent of their annual income every year, and virtually all employees were committed to do whatever was necessary to ensure the company continued to do well. It is noteworthy that all of the measures that resulted in efficiency gains and cost-savings over the past ten years had come from the work of JJJ's Operations Branch. For this and other reasons there was never any doubt that efficiency, effectiveness, and productivity gains would be compensated. JJJ was held in high esteem by all members of the IOMC Senior Management Committee.

Of course every boss has a boss. JJJ's boss was the CEO, Mike Brewmaster who supervised, in addition to the Chief Operating Officer, the Chief Financial Officer, the Chief Administrative Officer, and the Chief Audit Executive. Together they formed the IOMC Senior Management Committee. "The Brewster," as he was affectionately called, had been hired by the IOMC Board of Directors five years ago. A competent manager with an excellent track record at leading senior management teams, he was a caring and considerate boss, showing sympathy to the problems of his direct reports and always treating them with trust and respect. As far as making decisions, the Brewster liked the consensus/group decision approach and all of his direct reports did reasonably well under his leadership except for one: JJJ. While there were no outright "clashes" it was obvious to the rest of the senior management committee that the dynamic between the Brewster and J-Cubed was not always great—the latter thought the former took too long to make decisions (feeling perhaps he could not make *any* decisions on his own), that the decisions did not always require input from everyone (and certainly never consensus), and the company would be better served by the CEO focusing more on task and outputs, than on concern for his management team (who were, by all accounts, doing quite well).

One afternoon during a break in the management meeting JJJ's frustration boiled over.

"I can't believe this guy!" he said quietly to the Chief Audit Executive. "I have men and women out in the field doing real work under dangerous conditions. They are the entire backbone of this company—they always have been and always will be. They are looking to us for important decisions and leadership on the future, innovation, investments, research & development, safety improvements, etc. etc. and what does the Brewster want to discuss while he sips his mint tea? Some BS consultant's report written by a world-class BS'er who was paid an outrageous amount of money to tell us whether we should consider undertaking underwater basket weaving in the Bering Strait! What's worse, this no-brainer decision needs to be made by all of us! Can't Brewmaster just say 'no' all by himself, like any other normal Chief Executive?"

Robert Campbell, the Chief Audit Executive smiled, "actually Jim, it is about underwater *mining* which is, I grant you, a bit out of our league at the moment."

"Martin, you're amused by this" said JJJ. "But don't you remember the last 'séance' we had when the Brewster was trying to decide whether we should invest in the laser geomatics technology? That was classic 'decision-making by committee' at its finest. We spent all morning discussing it, and then we all agreed it was the way to go—perhaps because we were all *dying* by then and the Brewster *said* it was the way to go. So as the oxygen was running low in the boardroom we all decided 'yes' with our last breath, and what happened? The Brewster decides 'no', for some unknown reason, and ends the meeting. Well, he can't suck and blow at the same time—he either wants our input or not, and if not, fine—but then *make* the decision!"

"Sometimes there is value to making decisions by asking for input from everyone with a stake, and in this case if we decide to explore underwater mining you are the key stakeholder among us, I would say," replied Martin.

"Someone said once that a camel is a racehorse built by a committee. Look Marty, I'm only suggesting that every single management decision that needs to be made does not need to involve all of us. This is a no brainer—we are not tooled up even to explore this style of mining, the report indicates no proven reserves of anything we would even consider mining, and the risks are too high to our people even if this might be viable someday. And the Brewster knows this full well, so why waste all our time on this? Anyway, hey, if the Brewster wants to explore underwater mining in the Bering Strait I say we put some fins, a mask, and a mixed gas scuba air tank on the consultant, drop him over the side, let out one thousand feet of rope—and that's how deep it is there, by the way—and ask him to give two tugs on the rope if he sees anything shiny that's not a fish, and three tugs once he's got it all collected and wants to come up."

Questions

1. Analyze the leadership styles exemplified by Mike Brewmaster and JJJ.

2. Discuss how the differences in leadership styles might affect the IOMC.

The Fairborne Manufacturing Company Limited—Partners and the Corporate Raider

The Fairborne Manufacturing Company Limited (FMCL) was a manufacturer of complex printed circuit boards that ran cruise control modules in all major domestic and foreign automobiles. Originally founded by two brothers in 2001, Clinton and Maxwell Fairborne, both computer engineers, it started as a partnership; Clinton and Maxwell were general partners and were joined by Matthew Dent and William Ruddie. Dent supplied $180,000 of start-up cash to the company, was unknown to the public and took no active role in its management. Ruddie was a world-renown automobile designer who, in exchange for a share of profits, loaned his name to the partnership by way of endorsement, but like Dent, took no active management role.

In 2005, after continuous success and with greater manufacturing capacity needed, Clinton and Maxwell incorporated their business and after considerable legal manoeuvring, took FMCL public, selling shares to the public on the Toronto Stock Exchange (TSX). The initial public offering was a huge success, allowing fast expansion. This also complicated business operations as it soon became too large for the two brothers and their initial team of specialists to run. Clinton and Maxwell, or "C&M" as they became affectionately known, felt that a formal system of organization and administration was necessary to ensure efficiency and effectiveness. They decided to organize the business by setting up departments that were responsible for operations in different areas of the country as well as departments responsible for specific processes involved in producing the circuit boards. A third set of departments included finance, human resources, and legal services. Despite all the people they knew socially and with whom they had worked in the past, C&M also staffed each position based on performance and ensured that the authority and responsibility of each position relative to every other position was made clear.

As the corporation grew, it enjoyed increasing success—so much so that in 2015 it purchased one of its competitors, Sunmoto of Japan, also a producer of circuit boards for cruise control modules, usually found in heavy equipment applications. FMCL also enjoyed a solid reputation as an ethical company—C&M strongly believed that the actions of the company, while not always good for everyone affected, should at least result in the greatest good for the greatest number. Despite its continuing success, FMCL seemed not to pay sufficient attention to the actions of its competitors. In 2018, C&M and the FMCL Board of Directors were taken by surprise when its contracts with major automobile manufacturers were not renewed. As a result, its revenues fell sharply and its share price tumbled. As it happened, a newly organized company from Korea was providing the exact same product to the automobile manufacturers at a price 30 percent lower than FMCL.

By the end of 2018, FMCL was in a serious financial bind. Its share price had tumbled from a high of $156.50 in 2015 to a historic low of $28.50. To make matters worse, a notorious corporate raider was offering to buy all outstanding FMCL shares for $35.00 per share and was planning on securing the purchase with FMCL assets! C&M reacted by allowing its current shareholders to buy additional shares at $20.00 per share. As of mid-2019, the outcome and future of FMCL was uncertain.

1. When FMCL purchased Sunmoto of Japan in 2015, this was an example of a(an) _____merger.

2. Mathew Dent and William Ruddie would both be referred to as _____ partners; more specifically Dent would be a _____ partner while Ruddie would be a _____ partner.

3. In SWOT analysis, FMCL's failure to actively monitoring the actions of competitors means that they did not consider these actions a _____.

4. The corporate raider was attempting a _____ takeover, and by securing the purchase of FMCL shares with FMCL's own assets, this would be considered a _____ _____.

Downsizing The Apex Corporation (Part 1)

In early 2019, Bartholomew Banting, Senior Executive Vice President of the Apex Corporation, attended a meeting with the President and Chairman of the Board. This meeting was called to review the Corporation's financial performance. The President and Chairman of the Board, the Executive Vice President, and the Vice President of each of the major divisions constitute the senior management team.

The Apex Corporation is a Canadian telecommunications company, providing telephone services to Eastern Ontario and Northern Quebec. In addition to providing telephone services, the company also has satellite linkages with other networks and maintains a Research and Development Branch that manufactures satellites and performs continuous research in areas such as fibre optics and photonics. The Apex Corporation's financial performance is declining, as indicated by the financial reports provided by the Comptroller, and set out in the Appendices. Much of the financial decline is due to offshore competition and other effects of globalization.

The Apex Corporation is a unionized company with all nonmanagement employees represented by "TWA"—the Telecommunications Workers Association. The workers are governed by a single collective agreement, the current version of which provides employees with the right to strike under certain conditions.

Salaries and wages represent approximately 85 percent of the "Administrative Costs" and the union has been more or less supportive in keeping wage settlements down to slightly above the rate of inflation. The Apex Corporation is located in the town of Mintzberg, Ontario, where it is essentially the only employer. Within the company itself, employees are dispersed among four divisions, with each division headed by a Vice President (included in the "management employees."

Communications Division—Fifty Employees

The division sells, installs, and services the company's telephone and telefax network. This includes both wireless and landline services. Of the fifty employees, five are considered "management." Most of the workers are technicians with an average education level of high school graduation and earn an average salary of $48,000. While revenues from this division amount to 70 percent of total company revenues through the sale of its products, it represents 40 percent of the company's nonsalary administrative costs, 10 percent of the company's production costs, and 70 percent of the company's selling costs.

Production Division One Hundred Employees

This division produces telephone headsets, cellular devices, fax machines, and electronic parts. Ten of the hundred employees are considered "management." Most of the workers are assembly line workers who earn an average annual salary of $32,000. Because the products are sold to other divisions, this division does not generate external revenue, but rather supplies user departments with the goods to sell externally. This division represents 20 percent of the company's nonsalary administrative costs and 80 percent of the production costs.

Research and Development Division—Thirty Employees

The R&D division conducts research in fibre optics, photonics, and develops new technologies to keep the Apex Corporation competitive. This competitive edge is important, particularly in periods of economic slowdown and increasing competition from competitors from around the world. Three of the thirty employees are considered "management." The majority of workers in this division are well-qualified scientists and engineers commanding an average annual salary of $75,000. This division contributes 30 percent of the company's revenue through the direct sale of satellites, at a cost of 30 percent of the nonsalary administrative costs, 30 percent of the selling costs, and 10 percent of the company's production costs. This division is responsible for 80 percent of the company's research and development costs.

Administration Division—Twenty-Five Employees

This division includes Finance, Internal Audit, Legal, Human Resource Management, Material Management, Program Evaluation, and General

Administration units. Of the twenty-five employees, two are "management." Many of the employees have professional credentials (e.g., accountants, lawyers, auditors). The average annual salary in this division is $55,000. The division contributes nothing to revenue, generates no production costs, represents 10 percent of the company's nonsalary administrative costs, and 20 percent of the research and development costs.

The new fiscal year has started and the forecasted profits look grim. In addition, the union contract has expired and the union is seeking a 20 percent increase in wages, among other things. The Vice President of Research and Development has just informed the meeting that two major contracts worth $1.0 million and $1.5 million, respectively thought to have been "in the bag" may be lost to a competitor who was able to offer a considerably lower bid price. This revenue loss has *not* been reflected in the Comptroller's report (in other words, the revenue number reported in the Comptroller's report includes these two contracts).

A computer modelling application developed by the famous international consulting group Helo, Farmbent, and Roscoe (HFR, who were retained recently to undertake some preliminary cost analyses) has determined that production costs are fixed, but that selling, administration and research and development costs are variable and will decrease as staff decreases. Accordingly these "variable" costs can be expressed in terms of costs per employee, and for every person cut, a portion of these variable costs will decrease. HFR consultants have used the Comptroller's Reports in Annex A and Annex B to develop some numbers in this regard. These results are presented in Annex C.

HFR Consultants have conducted a number of analyses using complicated computer modeling and have determined that in order to avoid bankruptcy, the Apex Corporation must balance its 2019 budget and that means finding at least $4.0 million of savings. HFR Consultants together with the Comptroller undertaken exhaustive reviews in search of all areas in which costs could be reduced but have arrived at the conclusion that the $4.0 million can only be found in staff reductions. The senior management team at Apex has reluctantly agreed.

Given the reports prepared by the Comptroller, the constraint that the Production Division is exempt from this downsizing (as a result of the complex computer modelling program), and given its own reports provided in Annex C, HFR Consultants have put forth two options for downsizing:

1. A 25 percent staff reduction in each of Apex's divisions (except Production); or,

2. A 50 percent staff reduction in the Research and Development Division.

The Senior Management Team at Apex has decided that the recommendation on which option to implement should be taken by another external and objective group of consultants.

Required

Your team has been hired by the Apex Corporation to propose which one of the two downsizing options should be implemented and why. Assume that all computations are correct and that the options proposed by HFR are fully informed.

Annex A

The Apex Corporation
Comptroller's Report 1
Statement of Profit and Loss

	2015 $000's	2016 $000's	2017 $000's	2018 $000's	2019 Forecast $000's
Gross Revenues	26,700	24,400	28,000	22,000	23,500
Fixed Production Costs (25% of Revenues)	6,250	5,625	6,500	5,000	5,250
Variable Selling Costs (20% of Revenues)	5,000	4,500	5,200	4,000	4,200
Variable Nonsalary Administrative Costs (15% of Revenues)	3,750	3,375	3,900	3,000	3,150
Variable Research and Development Costs	1,700	1,900	2,000	2,000	2,500
Salaries and Wages Costs (excludes employee benefit costs)	6,100	6,400	7,200	8,100	10,000
Employee Benefit Costs (24% of S&W costs)	1,464	1,536	1,728	1,944	2,400
Pretax Profit/(Loss)	2,436	1,064	1,472	(2,044)	(4,000)
No. of Employees	160	160	170	180	205

The Apex Corporation
Comptroller's Report 2
Positions and Salary Costs by Division for 2019

Division	No. of Employees	Management	Nonmanagement	Salaries and Wages Cost ($000's)	Employee Benefit Plan Costs ($000's)
Communications	50	5	45	2,400	576
Production	100	10	90	3,200	768
R&D	30	3	27	3,000	720
Administration	25	2	23	1,400	336
Total	**205**	**20**	**185**	**10,000**	**2,400**

Annex B

The Apex Corporation
Comptroller's Report 3
Average Pay and Benefit Cost per Employee by Division (from Report 2)
For 2019
All Figures in $000's

Division	Average Salary per Employee	Employee Benefits Costs	Total Pay and Benefits Cost per Employee
Communications	48.0	11.5	59.5
Production	32.0	7.7	39.7
Research and Development	100.0	24.0	124.0
Administration	56.0	13.4	69.4

The Apex Corporation
Comptroller's Report 4
Nonpay Costs by Division
For 2019
All Figures in $000's (Except No. of Employees)

Division	No. of Employees	Production Costs		Administration Costs		Research and Development Costs		Selling Costs		Total Costs
		%	$	%	$	%	$	%	$	$
Communications	50	10	525	40	1,260	0	0	70	2,940	4,725
Production	100	80	4,200	20	630	0	0	0	0	4,830
Research and Development	30	10	525	30	945	80	2,000	30	1,260	4,730
Administration	25	0	0	10	315	20	500	0	0	815
Total	205	100	5,250	100	3,150	100	2,500	100	4,200	15,100

Annex C

HFR Costing Report for the Apex Corporation
Administration Costs Per Employee per Division (2019)*
$000's

Division	No. of Employees	Variable Nonsalary Administration Costs		
		%	$Cost	$Cost/Employee
Communications	50	40	1,260	25.2
Production	100	20	630	6.3
Research and Development	30	30	945	31.5
Administration	25	10	315	12.6
Total	**205**	**100**	**3,150**	

HFR Costing Report for the Apex Corporation
Research and Development Costs per Employee per Division (2019)
$000's

Division	No. of Employees	Variable Nonsalary Administration Costs		
		%	$Cost	$Cost/Employee
Communications	50	0	0	0
Production	100	0	0	0
Research and Development	30	80	2,000	66.7
Administration	25	20	500	20.0
Total	**205**	**100**	**2,500**	

HFR Costing Report for the Apex Corporation
Selling Costs per Employee per Division (2019)
$000's

Division	No. of Employees	Variable Nonsalary Administration Costs		
		%	$Cost	$Cost/Employee
Communications	50	70	2,940	58.8
Production	100	0	0	0
Research and Development	30	30	1,260	42.0
Administration	25	0	0	0
Total	**205**	**100**	**4,200**	

*Production costs are fixed and therefore not included in this cost analysis

HFR Costing Report for the Apex Corporation
Nonpay Variable and Pay Cost Savings for Each Employee Cut by Division*
2019
$000's

Division	Admin Costs per Employee	Research and Development Costs per Employee	Selling Costs per Employee	Total Nonpay Savings per Employee Cur	Average Salary and Benefit Savings per Employee Cut	Total Savings per Employee Cut
Communications	25.2	0	58.8	84.0	59.5	**143.5**
Research and Development	31.5	66.7	42.0	140.2	124.0	**264.2**
Administration	12.6	20.0	0	32.6	69.4	**102.0**

*Production costs are fixed and therefore not included in this cost analysis

HFR Costing Report for the Apex Corporation
Per-Employee Contribution to Revenue by Division (2019)
$000's

Division	No. of Employees	% of Company Revenue Generated	Amount of Company Revenue Generated	Revenue Generated per Employee
Communications	50	70	16,450	329.0
Research and Development	30	30	7,050	235.0
Administration	25	0	0	0

Note: The computer modelling confirms there will be no loss of revenue clearly attributed to decreasing the number of employees—a reduction in one employee will **NOT** translate into a loss of revenue generated per employee in the amount given in the table above.

The Apex Corporation (Part 2)— Downsizing: Which Manager Gets Let Go?

In early 20129, Bartholomew Banting, Senior Executive Vice President of the Apex Corporation attended a meeting with the President and Chairman of the Board. This meeting was called to review the Corporation's financial performance. The President and Chairman of the Board, the Executive Vice President, and the Vice President of each of the major divisions constitute the senior management team.

The Apex Corporation is a Canadian telecommunications company, providing telephone services to Eastern Ontario and Northern Quebec.

In addition to providing telephone services, the company also has satellite linkages with other networks and maintains a Research and Development Branch that manufactures satellites and performs continuous research in areas such as fibre optics and photonics. The Apex Corporation's financial performance is declining, as indicated by the financial reports provided by the Comptroller, and set out in the Appendices. Much of the financial decline is due to offshore competition and other effects of globalization.

HFR Consultants have conducted a number of analyses using complicated computer modeling and have determined that in order to avoid bankruptcy the Apex Corporation must balance its 2019 budget and that means finding at least $4.0 million of savings. HFR Consultants together with the Comptroller undertaken exhaustive reviews in search of all areas in which costs could be reduced but have arrived at the conclusion that the $4.0 million can only be found in staff reductions. The senior management team at Apex has reluctantly agreed.

A second team of consultants was retained to analyze and recommend one of the two possible courses of action proposed by HFR:

1. A 25 percent staff reduction in each of Apex's divisions (except Production); or,

2. A 50 percent staff reduction in the Research and Development Division

The Senior Management Team has decided that in addition to the outcome of Option 1 or Option 2 above, it must cut one senior manager in each division (other than Production).

Required

Your team has been hired by the Apex Corporation to make a rec-ommendation on which person from each division should be cut. The vitas of each affected manager are found in Annex A. Your task is to recommend which one of these persons in each division should be cut. You will need to develop a rationale to support your position.

Annex A

The Apex Corporation
Vitas of "Affected" Senior Staff

Communications Division

Roger Allison, age 46, married, two children. Allison has been with Apex for a year and a half. He is a very good engineer, with a degree from Rensselaer Polytech. He's held two prior jobs and lost both of them because of corporate downsizing exercises. He moved to Mintzburg from California to take this job. Allison is well liked by his coworkers.

LeRoy Jones, age 34, single. Jones is black and the company looked hard to get Jones because of Affirmative Action pressure. He is not very popular with his co-workers. Since he has been employed less than a year, not too much is known about his work. On his one evaluation (which was average) Jones accused his supervisor of bias against blacks. He is a graduate of Detroit Institute of Technology.

Research and Development Division

Donald Boyer, age 42, married, no children. Boyer is well liked by his coworkers. He has been at Apex five years, and he has a B.S., M.S., and Ph.D. in engineering from Purdue University. Boyer's ratings have been mixed. Some supervisors rated him high, some average. Boyer's wife is an M.D.

William Foster, age 53, married, three children. Foster has a Ph.D. in engineering from MIT. Twenty years ago he was hired at Apex by Bartholomew Banting, then a senior engineer in the R&D division. Foster is a likable person and popular with staff. His performance ratings were excellent for 15 years. The last five years they have been average.

Administration Division

Jacques Major, age 38, married, four children. Major is a Chartered Accountant with a MBA degree from the University of Ottawa. He is a hard worker and well regarded by the Comptroller. He has been with Apex for seven years, completing his MBA at night during that time. Apex reimbursed Major for the costs of his courses and gave him time off to study. Before joining Apex Major worked as a financial analyst for General Motors, but was let go as part of corporate restructuring. Major's performance appraisals have been excellent.

Sandra Chin, age 32, single. Chin is a qualified accountant in Canada, the United States and Hong Kong. She has a B.S. in Finance from Hong Kong Polytechnic, a MBA from Harvard and a MA in integrated risk management from the University of Toledo. Chin has been with the company for two years. She is regarded as a hard worker but has received only mediocre performance ratings since she join Apex. The Comptroller feels that she should be more of a team player and finds her extremely competitive. She is not particularly popular with the staff, but she is widely respected for her technical abilities.

The Kilowatt Electric Car Corporation

The Kilowatt Electric Car Corporation (KECC), founded in 2014 in Louisville, Kentucky was the manifestation of a vision held by five very wealthy businesspersons who saw the potential of the electric vehicle market as representing an essentially untapped market with enormous potential. The company was a privately held corporation, the shareholders of which wanted to run an efficient business that reflected the spirit of minimizing costs while preserving industry-leading quality in product and service.

KECC offered three vehicle designs that ran on three separate platforms. The KECC "*Electron*" was designed as a commuter and retailed for US$65,000. The KECC "*Megawatt*" was a high-performance, fully loaded luxury sedan that retailed for US$196,000. The KECC "*Electrocution*" was a high-performance, two-seater convertible sports car that retailed for US$129,000. Each model was successful.

Initially the company's focus was parochial: KECC was interested in developing a fully American-made electric automobile to serve the needs of high-income Americans. The company employed 300 persons at its corporate head office in Louisville, where its manufacturing plant was located. The company was organized as follows:

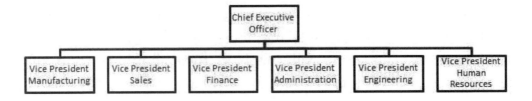

By 2019, KECC was doing extremely well with demand for its automobiles exceeding supply, with waiting lists approaching two years. In reviewing its performance, the senior management team made the following observations:

1. The demand for certain models was higher in certain geographic areas. For example, the main sales of the Electrocution were generally found in the southern states, Florida, South Carolina, Texas, and Southern California.

2. The greatest sales of the Megawatt were found in New York City, but also in Massachusetts, Connecticut, and Georgia.

3. Sales of the Electron were consistent across the United States.

4. Demand for all the KECC product offerings now extended to the United Kingdom, Spain, and the United Arab Emirates, although the company, up to this point, did not ship outside the United States.

Given this intel, the CEO is pondering whether to modify the organizational structure to better serve KECC clients. She is considering two possible options: geographic departmentalization or product departmentalization.

Required

Advise the CEO.

Marty's Mall Mart

In January, 2018, Martin Hayward took over the lease of a building previously occupied by a major retail specialty store located in a busy suburban mall in Hamilton, Ontario. The building was similar in size to those occupied by retail outlets such as Zellers. Martin wanted to transform this empty labyrinth into a fully functional department store that offered a variety of products.

Martin's business plan was very detailed and well thought-out. Marty's Mall Mart was the name under which business was carried on for 11911111 Ontario Inc., a private corporation incorporated under the laws of Ontario. Financing of the corporation was accomplished through a combination of equity (share capital) and debt (bank loans). Through the issue of common shares to twenty friends and family, Martin Hayward raised 65 percent of the capital requirements outlined in his business plan. The remaining 35 percent was obtained through bank loans and an operating line of credit. With the financing in place and the building leased for a three-year period, Martin began the daunting task of organizing his business.

Although Martin had worked for several years as a general manager for a major retail department store, he knew he needed to hire management expertise to complement his own skills, so he hired Robert Mitchell, an individual with over thirty years' experience as a retail manager to serve as his Executive Vice President and Marty's Mall Mart's General Manager.

Hayward and Mitchell decided to organize Marty's Mall Mart around the jobs that needed to be done, agreeing that, compared to many businesses, this business would reasonably expect to experience only modest growth calling for a stable organization structure. Hayward and Mitchell first created an administration division consisting of finance and accounting, human resource management, and marketing. Then, according to the business plan, they created a number of operational departments: men's clothes, women's clothes, shoes, hardware and automotive, music including audio and video equipment, toys, home and garden, small and large appliances, sports equipment, and furniture.

Each operational department would be headed by a department manager who would be responsible for managing the department. This would include full authority to staff the sales positions, assign tasks, monitor the performance of his or her staff, and delegate tasks to subordinates.

The organization structure would appear as presented in Figure 2 below. Hayward and Mitchell perceived that the operation of Marty's Mall Mart would occur through a combination of line and staff authority, however, whenever new products were being considered, or if changes were necessary to the way in which the organization was functioning, a project organization would be created.

Notwithstanding the organizational structure, Hayward and Mitchell would cochair regular meetings of all the store managers through which to review store operations and look for areas in which efficiency gains could be made. While every manager would be entitled to voice his or her opinion and make suggestions, Hayward and Mitchell would have final decision approval authority and their decision would be binding on every manager.

Martin Hayward was a strong believer in continuous learning and wanted to ensure that employees would continue to develop during their time at Marty's Mall Mart. He also believed that the investment in employee development would not only lead to happier, more effective, and efficient employees, but would also contribute to reducing turnover; a problem prevalent in the retail business. To assist in

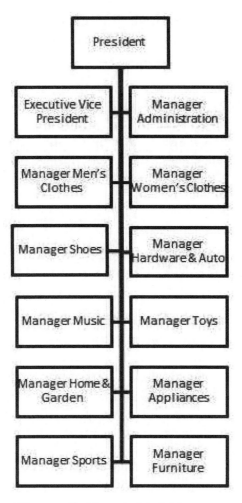

Figure II Marty's Mall Mart

employee development, Hayward put in place a policy that required every employee to follow a series of one-day seminars at which each manager would present his/her area of responsibility, describe how it works, what works well, the key challenges, and how it could be made to work better (with input from employee participants). The employees would receive full pay for participating at the seminars, and awards would be offered to employees who made suggestions at these seminars that lead to improvements in the operation of the store. Further, every employee would be encouraged to create new innovation that could be used by Marty's Mall Mart to build and sustain a competitive advantage.

Hayward believed in open channels of communication and tasked his managers with the responsibility to respond vigorously to any inaccurate information relating to the store or the people working there.

Required

Analyze Hayward's approach to organizing Marty's Mall Mart.

Water Street Optical

In January 2019, Mike Pritchard and Paul Smith were employed by Regency Optical Inc. Mike was an optician and Paul was the manager of a Regency Optical retail store located on Water Street in Toronto.

Regency Optical Inc. operated a number of retail optical dispensaries that sold fashion prescription eyewear, fashion sunglasses, and contact lenses. All of the company's retail outlets were leased; the leases, while long term, were operating leases. Of the three outlets that Regency operated, the Water Street location ranked lowest in terms of volume sales.

The optical industry is a relatively close-knit group in which the main participants are well-known among themselves. Most of the opticians in Toronto know each other; most of the dispensing optical outlet managers and employees know each other; most of the optical retail stores use the same suppliers. In this extremely aggressive competitive environment, the cost of inventory is usually differentiated only by volume discounts on inventory order. Personal customer service is very important because the selling price of eyewear is generally the same from one retail outlet to another. Success in this industry also depends on customer repeat business and a wide selection of inventory. Another factor of significance is the relatively low cost of purchasing inventory. Notwithstanding the Research and Development costs, depending on volume and the complexity of the prescription, contact lenses may cost the retailer $7 to $28, while eyeglass frames can range from $15 to over $100.

The president of Regency Optical Inc., Marcel Provost, was an aggressive "marketeer" who opted for increasing volume sales; in exchange, he settled for a lower profit margin on sales. The idea was to generate volume sales and use the cash profits as reinvestment funds to acquire more retail outlets. Advertising was aggressive and was undertaken centrally for all Regency's retail outlets. The longer-term plan was to develop scale economies such that Regency, because of volume alone, could offer to the public the most inexpensive frames at the highest possible quality. This strategy would perpetuate itself only if each Regency retail outlet experienced a certain threshold sales amount as determined by the management at Regency Optical Inc. For the Water Street location, this level of sales was established at $35,000 per month. Sales below this amount were not compatible with Regency Optical's overall plan.

In the first four months of operation, the Somerset Street location averaged $23,500 per month in sales, with its best month at $28,000. Because these results were well below the established sales threshold, the president of Regency decided to close Water Street and try a different location.

Paul Smith felt strongly that the Water Street location, if it were to cater more to customer service and offer the services of a stellar optician, could be made to meet the $35,000 per month threshold. The management at Regency Optical Inc. disagreed; they pointed out that despite its downtown location, Water Street did not attract a large enough client base.

Smith responded that perhaps the $35,000 threshold was only a theoretical amount; just because Water Street's performance was below this threshold did not necessarily mean that it was unprofitable. Regency management agreed that Water Street could be mathematically profitable, but its performance was not consistent with Regency's business plan.

Smith continued to feel strongly about the potential success of the Water Street location. Eventually, Regency agreed to sell the Water Street location to Smith for $160,000. Dewar would pay $60,000 cash and Regency would finance the remaining $100,000 over the next five years charging no interest. The price would include all inventory on hand at the time, and Smith's new business would assume responsibility for all outstanding Water Street liabilities. The agreement was finalized, and on April 1, 2019, Water Street Optical (WSO) was born.

Smith immediately launched his new business endeavour. As it already physically existed, he went to work the next morning as always, but now as an owner. Paying very little attention to the optimal type of business ownership, his first action was to register the business as a sole proprietorship—this was the most inexpensive option, and the simplest. He next opened new bank accounts, changed the store signs and started a rigorous advertising campaign. Mindful of the regulations governing optical dispensing, Smith then undertook an intensive campaign to hire an optician. During the search period, he made extensive use of optical laboratory services to fill the numerous orders that had resulted from his advertising efforts. Laboratory services, while offering timely and high-quality work, are relatively expensive; considerable savings can be had if the retail outlet can cut its own lenses.

In May 2019, Mike Pritchard left Regency Optical Inc. and joined WSO. A seasoned professional optician with a wide client base, Pritchard was well regarded as one of Canada's finest contact-lens fitters. He was also certified as a laboratory technician and could, therefore, cut lenses on site for WSO, avoiding the high laboratory costs. Pritchard offered his services for the going market rate—$60,000 per year—*plus a 50 percent ownership in Water Street Optical.* Smith accepted the offer. An effective retail manager, with skills in merchandising and advertising, and a certified optician appeared to be winning combination.

Instead of changing the provincial business registry, Pritchard and Smith prepared a contract that, among other things, described Mike as a partner and formalized the partners' respective salaries at $60,000 and $35,000.

As WSO began to enjoy steadily increasing sales and establish itself as a serious contender in the Toronto optical market, the president of Regency Optical had second thoughts about his decision to sell the outlet to Smith.

In July 2019, Marcel Provost paid a surprise visit to WSO. He was impressed with the store's look: a good mixture of high-quality frames and premium contact lenses, among other things. A steady stream of customers came through the door while he was there. In fact, he thought he recognized a few of his own customers!

Provost was indeed surprised to learn that WSO was averaging $46,000 per month in gross sales since they started the business on April 1st. In view of the deep discounts, WSO was offering its customers, had the goods been sold at full retail price, gross sales would have been double the amount reported. But Provost knew very well that no one ever paid the full retail price for eyewear. Even so, using the discount scheme offered by Regency Optical Inc. (which was not quite as deep as the one offered by WSO), the level of sales under the Regency scheme could be expected to gross at least $48,000 in monthly sales for WSO.

Provost suggested that Smith and Pritchard could benefit considerably by participating in the volume discounts available to Regency Optical Inc. He offered to take back 51 percent ownership of WSO, canceling the remaining debt owed WSO for the purchase agreement and refunding the $30,000 paid to Regency to date. In return, 51 percent of all profits from WSO would go to Regency Optical Inc. and the remaining 49 percent would be split between Smith and Pritchard. Furthermore, Provost would pay Pritchard a salary of $90,000 per year if he agreed to provide services to Regency's four existing locations. WSO would change its name to Regency Optical, but the partners could run the Water Street operation without interference from Provost.

Ever the pragmatic conceptual manager, Smith asked Provost to describe how his company was now organized. Provost described the organization of Regency Optical Inc. as follows:

"Reporting to the president (Provost) are the managers from each of the Regency Optical retail outlets, the central laboratory, and the corporate managers of administration, finance and accounting, marketing, and the external accountant (under contract as advisor and auditor). Reporting to each retail outlet manager is the optician(s). We also employ two physicians whose practices are limited to treatments of the eye. While operating as separate business entities, these practices report to the president of Regency. The doctors' receptionists report directly to the respective physicians. There is also an eye examination centre operated by an optometrist who reports directly to the president of Regency. Two of the four retail outlets are being restructured so that the manager will own 49 percent of the retail outlet. All stock orders, bills, and leasing matters are dealt with centrally and administered by Regency Optical's corporate downtown location.

The central optical laboratory is located in the retail outlet in the east end of the city. Regency employs at least two opticians per location, and at least five full-time and four part-time sales clerks. There is also a delivery person who delivers stock orders to the respective locations. This delivery person reports to the president. All capital equipment is centrally leased and dispersed to each location. In addition, the opticians can work in any of the locations with the approval of the president. The marketing manager handles all leasehold details and all advertisements on behalf of all locations. All accounting functions are centralized at the downtown location. The profit structure is different for each store depending on each manager's personal investment in his or her retail outlet, and none of the proposed 51 percent to 49 percent ownership splits have been legally established. This structure provides for maximum flexibility and maximum growth potential."

After Provost left, Smith and Pritchard called their consultant and relayed the above information and "offer," seeking her advice on whether the offer was a good one or not.

Required

You are the consultant. Advise Smith and Pritchard whether to make the deal.

Governance at the Ronin Utilities of Inner Newfoundland (RUIN) Corporation

Dave "Big Foot" Cordell was the CEO of Ronen Utilities of Inner Newfoundland (RUIN) Corporation. Since deregulation of the oil, gas, and hydro industries in the 1980s Cordell had put together an enormously successful publicly traded utilities company that had become the blue chip "darling" of investors. Offering returns on investment far above the industry norm for over twenty years, several pension funds and other institutional investments were heavily invested in RUIN shares. Over the years, RUIN had amassed a large and experienced board of directors consisting of the CEO, academics, lawyers, engineers, accountants, and experienced business manager who were geographically dispersed internationally. The CEO was the Chairman of the Board and "ruled the roost." Except for the CEO, each board member was paid $450,000 per year. Members of the board of directors were participants on several key committees including the finance committee, legal committee, and audit committee. RUIN adhered to all external financial reporting requirements by relying on the public accounting firm of Jim, Slim, and Dim, LLP who occupied two floors of the RUIN building. RUIN paid annual accounting and consulting fees to the public accounting firm of $50,000,000 per year.

In late 2018, Bob Bolivar, an internal auditor and certified public accountant, in the course of an audit on internal control systems, stumbled across some transactions he thought were somewhat obscure and irregular. He noticed a pattern whereby twenty-four hours before every major announcement that would have the effect of either increasing or decreasing the market value of RUIN shares, the CEO and other members of the board of directors either purchased or sold some of their personal share holdings. Further, he discovered two instances where nebulous accounting practices significantly overstated company earnings.

After bringing this to the attention of the CEO, he was told "not to worry about it because if anything was wrong the external accountants would have found this." Dissatisfied, he raised his findings with Slim Creditmeister, a partner in Jim, Slim, and Dim, LLP. Slim promised to look into it, but even after three weeks Bolivar had heard nothing. Frustrated, Bolivar sent an anonymous email message to the Canada Revenue Agency who launched an immediate investigation. The outcome of this investigation proved the following findings:

- earnings were indeed materially overstated in several years,
- the CEO and some members of the board of directors made personal gains directly attributed to the timing of the sale and purchase of RUIN shares for their personal investment portfolios,
- RUIN had been taking exorbitant financial risks by debt financing expensive and high-risk oil and gas explorations in the Arctic, securing RUIN debt instruments with RUIN shares that were at least 65 percent overstated due to the improper accounting practices.

Apparently, these improper accounting practices were never discovered by the external auditors. RUIN declared bankruptcy in 2019.

Required

Respond to the following questions:

1. Given the circumstances at RUIN, which one of the following four groups of stakeholders has been most negatively affected?

    a. Shareholders

    b. Board of Directors

c. Management

d. Employees

2. Which one of the following is the most negative aspect of corporate governance practices at RUIN?

   a. The use of outside directors

   b. The use of board committees comprised of board members

   c. The use of internal auditors

   d. The CEO as de-factor chairman of the board

3. The term that best describes the CEO's and board members' practice of purchasing or selling shares immediately before announcements that would affect the market price of the RUIN shares is called:

   a. Greenmail

   b. Insider trading

   c. Poison pill

   d. Golden parachute

4. The group that bears the greatest responsibility for the failure of RUIN is:

   a. The board of directors

   b. The CEO

   c. Shareholders

   d. RUIN senior management

5. Which one of the following fiduciary duties typically ascribed to members of boards of directors, was inarguably breached by some of the directors of RUIN?

   a. To consider other shareholders

   b. To declare conflicts of interest

    c. No personal profits at company expense

    d. None of the above

6. Bob Bolivar is a "whistleblower."

    a. True

    b. False

Exclusive Limousine Ltd.

Exclusive Limousine Ltd. (ELL) of Cornwall was established in 2001 as an upscale transportation option for corporate executives, diplomats and visiting dignitaries, and movie stars. In almost twenty years of operations, ELL had done very well financially and had established an impeccable service record. The majority of ELL's staff had been with the company since its inception including its management team as well as twenty of its twenty-five full-time chauffeurs.

Its current fleet of limousines included a range of custom-made Cadillacs, Lincolns, Bentleys, and Rolls Royce that were always in demand, particularly to and from the Cornwall International Airport.

Notwithstanding its history of success, ELL's fuel expenses are increasing and in a volatile way: every week the average cost of fuel fluctuates—usually upward. This is becoming a significant challenge for the management team, as it is reluctant to operate on a system of fluctuating fares, preferring instead to modify fares annually as part of their planning process. To operate on a system of fluctuating fares would, in the words of ELL's CEO, "turn ELL into a high-end cab company." The volatility of fuel costs also affects ELL in other ways, including the increasing costs of parts for the maintenance and repair of its fifty-limousine fleet.

Rodney Barrington was recently hired as ELL's Chief Planning Officer with a mandate that included, among other things, "to look into, and plan for, the future of ELL." One of the initiatives he was exploring was the conversion of the fleet vehicles to liquefied natural gas instead of the gasoline and diesel currently in use. The CEO was open to learning more about the initiative and has asked Rodney to "fully develop a comprehensive plan to convert the fleet vehicles," noting that this plan must be anchored in costs, environmental concerns, stakeholder interests, "and any other factors that will help the board of directors make an informed decision."

Required

Prepare a plan for the CEO.

Huang Chow Enterprises

In early 2019, the Chinese company Huang Chow Enterprises (HCE) developed a silicon chip that stacked ten thin wafers resulting in a chip that ran twenty times faster than anything on the market anywhere in the world. The "Dix Chip" was only a prototype and would require further testing in advanced computer systems in order to validate the new technology as reliable. The next challenge would be to make the chip commercially viable in advanced systems around the world.

Mr. Richard Chow, the President of the state-owned HCE, and Dr. Lisa Chung, HCE's Director of Research and Development and the brains behind the Dix Chip, felt that to bring this technology to wide commercial application HCE would need to establish strategic partnerships with leading edge firms in key G-8 countries. However, they also believed that establishing strategic partnerships would be most effective if they started with one country. Richard Chow, who had traveled extensively and had several contacts in countries around the world, believed that Canada would be the best country with which to start, not because of any intimate knowledge of Canadian business practices or its economy, but rather because of his respect for many new Canadian advanced technology developments and applications that he read about during 2017 and 2018.

It was decided that Mr. Chow and Dr. Chung would travel to Canada to discuss the details of their technology and the opportunity for strategic partnership with a personal friend of Dr. Chung's, Dr. Michael Smith, the President of the University of the Rocky Mountains, a highly regarded university dedicated entirely to engineering and technology pursuits and one that boasted three world-class technology research facilities. Smith agreed to see Chow and Chung, and invited Warren Gifford, the President and CEO of Chip Tech Technologies, a highly successful Canadian silicon chip development company with subsidiary operations in the United States, Mexico, and Europe.

In preparing for the meeting, Chow and Chung developed a number of slides through which to present their technology as well as what they perceived to be the parameters of a strategic partnership for the further development of the technology. Selected slides from their presentation are given below.

GOAL OF THE STRATEGIC PARTNERSHIP

To further develop the Dix Chip to be commercially applied to all computer applications

To promote the use of the Dix Chip in all computer and related technology applications across the G-8 countries

---

PARTNERS

LHE and the government of the PRC

University of the Rocky Mountains

Chip Tech Technologies

SUMMARY OF DETAILS

Intellectual property rights to be retained by LHE and the government of the PRC who would also provide all necessary capital investments and approve all aspects of the research and application, including employees assigned

The price of the chip to be charged by LHE in Canada and the United States would be determined and fixed by LHE and the government of the PRC and would be set intentionally low to allow for market penetration

---

SUMMARY OF DETAILS

The University of the Rocky Mountains to receive a generous funded research grant of $5,000,000 to help with the Quattro Chip's development

Chip Tech Technologies to receive a commission of 5% on all commercial sales of the chip for 3 years

The meeting was held at the University of the Rocky Mountains on 4th February 2019. While Chow and Chung believed this would be perceived as an outstanding opportunity for both the University and Chip Tech Technologies, the reception, while professional, was not what they expected. After listening to the 20-slide presentation, Warren Gifford began.

"Mr. Chow and Dr. Chung, we are honoured that you would think of Chip Tech as a worthy partner in your effort to commercialize the Dix Chip, and while your technology appears to be quite promising, I'm afraid that what you propose in terms of ownership of the intellectual property and pricing is not acceptable."

"Lisa," began Dr. Smith, "doing business in this country and countries with a similar approach to business and economics is quite different from what you are accustomed to. We subscribe to free ownership of the factors of production and believe that price should be determined in accordance with the laws of supply and demand. Further, in recent years there has been a strong movement toward deregulation with the government becoming increasingly less involved in owning business enterprises. What you propose in this strategic partnership is entirely at odds with current business practices and philosophy."

"As well," said Gifford with a smile, "we prefer that government is not involved *at all* in our business operations—*any* government for that matter."

Richard Chow began slowly: "Gentlemen, I understand that our economic systems have different goals and our approaches are quite different, but are we not out for the same ultimate goal? You will appreciate that with the government of the PRC owning and controlling HCE, to propose a strategic partnership that would exclude the PRC government would be quite impossible."

"Unless of course *our* government became involved at the political level to help appease any concern the government of the PRC might have," suggested Michael Smith. "I know this might sound somewhat contradictory but notwithstanding our preference for no government involvement, the government can be useful for our purposes in certain roles."

"Even if the government's interest in this technology could be diminished, there still remains much negotiation to undertake," said Warren Gifford. "Assuming your government agrees to take a hands-off approach to this, we would still need to explore a more realistic arrangement for the ownership of intellectual property rights, particularly given the amount of additional R&D that will be necessary to make this chip commercially viable. A 5 percent commission on the sales of chips will not even come close to what my company would need to become involved in this project. And with respect to the price, the price should be whatever we can get for it, not "prescribed" or fixed."

Arthur Cox

Arthur Cox was the new manager of the Regina branch of the Winnipeg Construction Company (WCC). WCC was founded in 1905 in Winnipeg, Manitoba and had branch offices in many cities across Canada. Cox was recruited from a competing Canadian construction company six months ago, to replace the retiring manager of the Regina Branch, Paul Meech.

WCC was a successful company and its Regina branch had been its top performer until the last two years when its revenues continued to fall. Meech attributed this to considerably more competition in the construction area, particularly from American firms located in Minnesota and North Dakota. With the strength of the US dollar the affect of which was "to operate in Canada with a 35 percent discount" according to Meech, in his view it was becoming increasingly difficult to compete.

A mild-mannered and articulate man, Meech was a well-respected and highly effective professional administrator; a graduate of a major American business school, his approach to operations was to *"let the specialists specialize"* in other words, he was not a construction engineer, but the person responsible for that division was, so let that person manage the division. His job was to strategically manage the branch, not to tell the engineer how to build the structures, and although he knew his way around construction, the idea of him giving technical instructions to the engineer would be, in his words, *"like having a dentist tell a cardiac surgeon how to perform a heart transplant."*

Born and raised in Regina, he started at the newly established WCC Regina Branch shortly after graduation, satisfying his passion for construction and administration. Three years later he was appointed as the manager of WCC's Regina Branch, where he remained for the last thirty-eight years. It was under Meech's leadership that the Regina Branch became the most successful branch of WCC. In addition to being the highest profit-generating branch, the Regina Branch also had the lowest employee turnover and as it grew, had no difficulty in attracting the most qualified workers and management employees from across the world.

Meech was a very confident and affable person, who believed strongly in developing an environment in which his employees would become self-motivated. He encouraged all staff to voice their opinions in a professional way, without concern for adverse reaction from the management. He was charismatic and believed in, and demonstrated delegation and empowerment. He was a cautiously optimistic risk-taker who earned employees' respect and loyalty by sharing his managerial knowledge and providing them opportunities to grow and develop.

Cox's style and disposition was, to put it mildly, quite different from Meech. Cox was a construction worker who had risen through the ranks with a competing firm, serving as the firm's assistant manager before being recruited by WCC. In his prior role as Assistant Manager, Cox was directly responsible for managing the thirty-five construction workers that formed one-quarter of the staff at the competing firm. He was task-oriented, actively assertive, and was accustomed to exercising control and influence. He had a track record of always "making the numbers" that included, among other things, managing the wage budget of the workers.

Cox had started in the construction business twenty-two years ago at the age of twenty-three after completing a civil engineering degree at a major Canadian university. The company from where Cox was recruited, was his fifth construction company.

The management team at the Regina Branch of WCC was mutli-cultural, made up of Ray Nagawa, Chief of Engineering, Sheryl Morton, Chief of Sales and Marketing, Horst Kruger, Chief of Finance and Administration, and Alexandre Dubois, Chief of Quality Control. Cox also had an Executive Assistant, Michal Brown.

Ray Nagawa was born and raised in Japan where he earned his undergraduate degree in civil engineering from the Tokyo Institute of Technology. He subsequently completed a Master's degree in architecture from the Rhode Island School of Design. He had served in his position for ten years and was responsible for engineering, construction, and transport, with a staff of eighty.

Sheryl Morton was born and raised in Los Angeles and held earned degrees in business administration and marketing management from Harvard and Cornell universities. After working for ten years as a marketing manager for a major American construction and development company, she moved north. That was fifteen years ago. Morton had a staff of twenty employees, ten of whom were salespersons paid on commission.

Horst Kruger was born, raised and educated in Berlin, Germany. He held an undergraduate degree in Accounting Science and a Master's degree in Finance from the Cologne Business School, and had worked for ten years as an Accounting Manager for a major public accounting firm in Munich. Kruger was responsible for all the internal and external accounting of the Regina branch, including finance, contracts, and internal audit.

Horst's staff consisted of a senior assistant, six accounting clerks, and a secretary.

Alexandre Dubois was an internationally recognized expert in quality control. Born and raised in Lyon, France, Dubois held the French equivalent of an undergraduate and Master's degree in quality engineering from the Universities of Paris and Marseilles. He had worked for ten years for two major quality assurance consultancy firms in France. Dubois joined WCC Regina eight years ago and now headed a team of twelve inspectors.

Unlike Meech, Cox liked to start his weeks off very early and had a management meeting, what he called "a naval gazing" every Monday morning at 6:30 a.m. This morning's meeting was extremely important because Horst had recently tabled his financial reports, showing that the Regina branch of WCC was continuing to lose money—*"continuing to hemorrhage money"* were his exact words. Added to the financial worries, nine persons has resigned—noteworthy because in the past thirty-eight years under Meech, the only resignations that occurred were for retirement or relocation. To make matters worse, Sales and Marketing reported earlier in the week that several long-term Milcroft commercial contracts worth $1,500,000 had been lost to an American competitor, apparently attributed to "less than competitive pricing." Cox was concerned that senior WCC leadership would think this was his fault and he was concerned—he needed a solution and for this, he needed to lead and motivate his management team. He raised the matter with his team on Monday morning.

"Look folks, after only six months of my appointment your lacklustre management approach has put me in the very difficult position of having to explain this continuing hemorrhaging of money to my handlers in Winnipeg. Now I *will* to get to the bottom of this, and I am fully prepared to sit here all day if necessary. Kruger has finally provided his financial report which clearly shows an enormous quarterly operating loss. I assume the figures are correct, but I'll have Mike check the arithmetic just to be certain. And I hope there are no errors, Kruger! As for the rest of you, I would like to hear your thoughts on why we are having these continuous financial problem."

Sheryl Morton spoke first. "Mr. Cox, the impact of losing the commercial contracts has undoubtedly caused this operating loss. As I indicated in my report, the loss of these contracts was simply because we were not able to price match the American company due to the favourable exchange rates, and…"

"Look Sheryl," interrupted Cox, "I really don't give a hoot about all your fancy marketing explanations. The bottom line is that you're paid as a sales and marketing professional to figure out how to combat any type of marketing tactic. I want solutions that will work, not a pile of theoretical gobbledy-gook. I want you to fix the situation NOW, and don't allow this company to lose any more contracts. Do whatever is necessary." Arthur stared hard at Sheryl, shook his head and gazed toward the ceiling lifting his arms over his head, and said, "Look, you wanted a man's job, you somehow broke through the glass ceiling—good for you, congratulations! Now deliver!!"

Ray couldn't resist a slim smile. "You know, Mr. Cox," began Nagawa, "these are difficult economic times. Perhaps it would be in the best interests of the company and this management team to take a lower margin on certain contracts and at least generate some revenues, as opposed to maintaining our regular prices and losing additional contracts. We have to think about what is best for us, for our team…"

"So now, in addition to being an engineer, you are also an expert on pricing, sales, and accounting!" Cox leaned across the table within about six inches of Ray's face and said, "Look, Nagawa, I pay you to worry about transporting concrete and building structures so they don't fall down. We'll let Kruger worry about the bean counting, and sweet *Sherry* can worry about the sales and contracts. You just make sure my structures don't fall down!"

Ray folded his hands on the documents in front of him and looked down and away from Cox, without saying anything.

Monsieur Cox, I would like to raise a concern I have regarding the number of recent resignations," said Alexandre Dubois as Cox leaned back in his chair.

"Look, Dubois, I really don't think this is an appropriate time to discuss this issue. We are facing serious financial problems, *une catastrophe majeure* as you would say back in your country! The fact that a few people have resigned might actually save us enough dough to offset some of this loss!"

"But Monsieur Cox!" continued Dubois undaunted, but with a somewhat raised voice, "these were long-time staff members who knew the company and whose daily contributions cannot be replaced merely by reassigning tasks! And as far as replacing them, you will know there is a considerable learning curve…"

"LOOK!" roared Arthur Cox, "I am not interested in hearing any more bleeding heart stories or dimestore psychobabble. Everyone is replaceable, including you Dubois, and every other member of this country club so-called management team. Now the bottom line is this—before the end of the day, I want each of you to prepare a report on how you will operate your respective sections after I impose a 30 percent staff reduction. I want written suggestions on what I should tell head office. I want all of you to understand— your careers are on the line and you're betting your pay cheque on your suggestions! I am not happy with the performance of this team. From what I see around this table I don't know how they manage even to get water flowing down hill in Germany, Japan, and France, but I do know that THIS is how I manage in Canada, and if I have to change this team and replace everyone with *Canadian* managers, I will!"

"Now look people, we have work to do. We're all in this together. If you need any further direction, come and see me. My door is always open…."

Northern Alkaline Battery Recycling Company Ltd.

The Northern Alkaline Battery Recycling Company Limited (NABR) is located in Thomson Manitoba. The company is Canada's largest recycler of alkaline batteries and employs hundred families. With continuous demands to meet stricter environmental regulations combined with the need to invest in newer technologies to assist in the breakdown of the batteries, NABR financial viability is increasingly in question. There is a need to use every possible ways and means to reduce costs.

Recycling alkaline batteries requires the use of a chemical process to extract zinc, carbon, and manganese from the batteries. NABR recently discovered that a new toxic substance, dubbed "compound zephr," is by-product of the chemical process in use. More problematic is that compound zephr (CZ) cannot be recycled and must be disposed of.

CZ is generated in a powder form that in high concentrations, is particular toxic to fish and other marine creatures. To dispose of CZ properly would require the purchase of very expensive equipment for which NABR does not have the capital. The provincial government is not yet aware of the existence of CZ, but NABR biologists have determined that CZ is only extremely dangerous when not diluted—the more diluted the CZ becomes, the less toxic it is.

It happens that NABR's plant is located beside a river that has been declared dead by federal and provincial biologists. The source of the original pollution is a manufacturer of fertilizer that is located ten miles upriver from NABR. This company is still before the courts, fighting the court's recent judgement to cease and desist dumping waste material into the river. All the water that flows by NABR cannot support life due to its toxicity.

Rodney Burrows, the CEO of NABR, knows that if forced to dispose of the CZ "properly," NABR would go bankrupt because the cost of the equipment is prohibitive. This would have a catastrophic effect on the employers, shareholders, and other stakeholders. He has wondered whether NABR would be acting irresponsibly by discharging the CZ into the "already dead" river, particularly since the diluting effect of the river water would render the CZ less toxic.

Required

Advise Rodney Burrows.

Stromboni Racecar Corporation

Robert Frobisher gazed out his office window that overlooked downtown Toronto. It was dusk and the view was fabulous. But Robert was preoccupied. How things had changed in the ten years he was Vice President of Communications and Customer Relations for the Stromboni Racecar Corporation!

"There was a time when long-term planning was actually 'long-term'," he lamented to himself. "Nowadays, long term is weeks and short term is hours. Everyone wants an immediate answer to questions for which an immediate answer is simply not possible! Incidents happen and social media puts them in everyone's face instantaneously—there is no time to plan or think anymore, only to react and hope you get it right!"

With a huge sigh he slumped into his chair thinking about next steps to deal with a public relations crisis that had been brought public only minutes ago. Stromboni's star race car driver, Dominique Lacasse, had failed a drug test and was publicly disqualified from winning his last three races, pending further investigation.

Lacasse was the poster boy for Stromboni. In the last thirty races he lost only two. He was active in the community, volunteering at food banks, coaching children at the go-cart facilities, and guest lectured on many occasions at the local community college.

Frobisher reflected on how these things come out of nowhere with virtually no warning and cause a redefinition of crises management. How could any manager plan for these types of crises? It's not like planning a retreat, or setting operational goals—this is entirely different. How could he plan for a crisis?

Kevin's Mobile Frozen Yoghurt

In 2015, Kevin Calisle purchased a cubed van and converted it into a refrigerated 'rolling frozen yoghurt stand' travelling throughout the streets of greater Ottawa selling frozen yoghurt products. Over the next two years his reputation and success sky-rocketed to the point where he could no longer meet the demands for his product.

Calisle decided to expand his company by investing in three "leading edge" electric vans. These vans were completely electric—electricity ran the engines and the refrigerator units; they were environmentally clean and almost noiseless while operating on the streets. Most impressive was that a computer controlled everything from the refrigerator units to the onboard GPS that could identify the physical locations of all three units simultaneously.

By summer of 2019, Kevin had three electric vans in operation and had hired two additional drivers/servers. In addition to Yoghurt, he branched into coffee. This required a modification to the "electronics" that provided for the operation of both the refrigerator units on the one hand, and the heating elements for the coffee on the other. It was a marvel of engineering made possible by the "snap chip"—a proprietary computer chip manufactured and designed by the Gilcrist Corporation of Kanata. The snap chip was house externally, in a weatherproof plastic box sealed with silicon "o-rings' and mounted on the undercarriage of the van.

The Gilcrist Corporation designed both the chip and the weatherproof plastic box, and had the specifications for the o-ring sealing gasket transmitted to an American firm for manufacture. The American firm advised Gilcrist that the o-ring gasket was temperature sensitive, designed to operate in warm weather, and the probability of gasket failure increased as the temperature decreased. The American engineers provided the following technical information to Gilcrist:

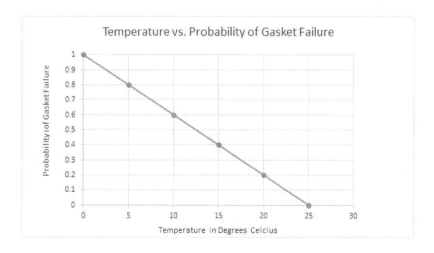

Typically, temperature was never an issue for Kevin as the majority of his yoghurt business occurred during the summer months. However the developing coffee market was expanding and in high demand. Kevin supplied his coffee regularly to businesses, in particular automobile repair garages and dealerships across the city, who continuously mentioned to him that they would like him to continue supplying coffee as long as possible into the fall. It was now September 1st. Coffee sales were an important source of revenue that would certainly assist him in paying off his creditors for the vans as well as the shareholders of his private corporation who expected a return on investment.

Kevin contemplated the weather report for the next four weeks that reflected the following forecast:

Period	Average Temp (Celsius)
1 September–15 September	26
16 September–30 September	23
1 October–15 October	21
16 October–31 October	20
1 November–15 November	15
16 November–30 November	12

Source: David Delcorde

The complicating factor was that due to his specialized insurance coverage, the costs would increase and he would not be able to add the insurance on a week-by-week basis, due to the stipulation of his policy. If he was to continue the vans beyond September 15th (the usual shut-down time), he would need to pay insurance up to and including December 31st. Even with the increased insurance cost, he was certain he could make a profit.

In reading the engineering report, Kevin noted that the failure of the o-ring could result in a malfunction of the electrically assisted power steering unit that would cause the steering to lock in place. In his "cautious" view, the probability of a steering wheel lock would be the same as the probability of the gasket failure, notwithstanding the engineering reports claim that even with a gasket failure it was not certain that the steering lock would occur.

Kevin contemplated whether he should continue operating his vans to 31st October.

Required

1. You are Kevin Carlisle. Would you operate to October 31st or park your vans on September 15th?

Human Resources Cases

Human resources cases range from exploring a given aspect of the human resources process (such as, for example, recruiting) to the development of an entire human resources management system.

Case Title	General Area of Focus	Page No.
Hiring Practices at Shelby's Security Systems Inc.	Recruitment and selection, discrimination	153
Martin Parks	Employee legacy, gender differences	154
Bert's Fine China Company Limited	Employee incentive systems	156
Cardiac Ken	Performance appraisal	159
Sunsilva Corporation	Tests	163
Antonio Cerveza and Cerveza Custom Jewellery Inc.	Labour-management relations	164

Hiring Practices at Shelby's Security Systems Inc.

In early 2019, retired police officer Jacques Shelby started his own private security company, *Shelby's Security Systems Inc.* (JSSI) with the proceeds of his severance pay. Jacques Shelby, who stood six foot five inches tall and weighed in at 260 pounds had been in enough scrapes during his thirty-year career in law enforcement to know the importance of physical size. In setting up his company, he wanted to recruit people "who could handle themselves physically."

In response to an employment opportunity advertisement placed by JSSI, several applications were received. The short list, based on a resume screening included Samantha Ross, Jean Pilon, and Suji Takahashi. Each candidate had previous security experience taken courses in security services. The advertisement did not provide any details on minimum size or gender.

Samantha Ross had completed a security management course at a local college and was working for a competitor as a security advisor. Shelby disqualified her after the interview saying, *"my security assignments are very dangerous and not suitable for a woman."*

Jean Pilon had completed training at a local police college but never became a police officer, preferring instead to study security management. He had experience working as a freelance security guard, but at five foot six inches did not fit Jacques' stereotype of a security guard. Shelby thought that Jean *"...was too scrawny and besides, his English language skills were not the best."*

Suji Takahashi stood a paltry five foot two inches and weighed 136 pounds. Fluent in three languages with a college diploma in security and a Bachelor degree in criminology, he also was an accomplished martial artist holding black belts in Judo, Karate, and Tai Kwon Do. According to Shelby, Suji *"...did not fit the mould of a security guard and would not instil the same confidence in clients as a larger man."*

Martin Parks

Martin Parks (MP) had been employed by Dudley Industries Inc. for ten years as a senior secretary. He had a track record of highly complimentary performance appraisals during his tenure reporting to the Vice President of Public Relations.

Three months ago, MP was reassigned to Susan Gilchrest, Vice President of Operations for Dudley Industries Inc. (Dudley), following the retirement of the Vice President of Public Relations. Susan was thirty-eight years old and held an undergraduate degree in electrical engineering from the Massachusetts Institute of Technology (MIT) and an MBA from Harvard. She had joined Dudley Industries Inc. as Vice President, Operations, having been recruited from a competing firm four years ago, and served in a number of key positions during her rise through the ranks. MP would be her third secretary during her time at Dudley.

The Operations Sector of Dudley was a very pressure-filled environment with ongoing production deadlines, and constant meetings with the suppliers of the many components the company needed to produce its newest and highly successful innovative marvel of information communications technology—the *widget*. Attention to detail in this environment was particularly important, given the importance of the widget to the longer-term sustainable competitive advantage of Dudley and the relentless competition that is typical in most industries, but very acute in the information communications technology sector.

Three months ago, MP was keen to take on new challenges however recently the quality of his work had steadily declined. Last Wednesday Susan had been on the receiving end of a less than flattering "blast" from the Executive Vice President for a plethora of spelling and grammatical errors that had appeared in a final report on the status of the Operations Department that was to be presented to the President and Chairman of the Board of Directors. To make matters worse, a production report had been sent to the President with three pages missing—fortunately caught in time by the President's Executive Secretary.

MP always seemed to be *dancing to the beat of a different drummer*, as some of his colleagues said. He was rarely in the office on time, took frequent breaks, missed work without calling in, and frequently called in sick at very busy times.

This morning Susan thought it was critical that she discuss her concerns with MP. In the meeting Susan voiced her dissatisfaction with MP's work and wanted to learn from him whether there were any particular circumstances causing the deterioration of his work, and whether she could help.

MP had simply replied, *"Look Susan, I've been around this place a lot longer than you, and in the past few years I've put out my pound of flesh. I started in the mailroom and progressed quite well despite my lack of academic memorabilia to hang on the wall. My record is spotless and I've survived lots of tough times while working for some very demanding male managers. So if I seem somewhat slack from time to time, I've earned it. Besides, what's stopping you from hiring a student to proofread these reports? It would be a great job for a summer for COOP student and would free me up to do more important things for this department."*

Questions

You are Susan Gilchrest. How would you handle this situation?

Bert's Fine China Company Limited [17]

Located in Chelsea, Quebec, the Bert's Fine China Company Limited (BFCC) was founded in 1850 by Jimmy Delaney and operated as a family-owned and family-run business until 1950 when it grew into a

---

[17] Case written by Dr. David H J Delcorde, Telfer School of Management, University of Ottawa, 2011, updated 2019. Inspired by Smith Rubber, appearing in The Excalibur (2003), The Canadian University Tournament of Human Resources.

medium-sized company requiring more sophisticated management than was available from among the family shareholders. Notwithstanding its local history, it is now facing considerable competition locally and internationally. Until recently it has been able to compete with Canadian companies as well as medium-sized American companies in supplying consumer and commercial demand for fine china. Martin Best is now the CEO of BFCC and has served as its CEO since 2005. Given the evolving state of the market, Best is considering the best approach to increasing efficiency and productivity without offering a wage increase that would ultimately increase his fixed costs as well as liabilities to the company pension plan that is tied to payroll costs. In 2018 the company had a tremendously successful year and this resulted in providing a bonus to all employees. The company followed a fiscal year that ran from 1st October to 30th November and the bonuses were paid on December 15th.

BFCC Bonus System Fiscal Year 2017–18

Salary Rage ($)	Amount of Bonus
40,000 and under	$3,000
40,001–50,000	$3,500
50,001–60,000	$4,000
60,001–70,000	$4,500
70,001 or higher	15% of salary

The employees were thrilled with this unexpected bonus and as a result, many employees were motivated to work harder in anticipation of even greater bonuses in the future. In 2019, however, the market changed dramatically—sales fell by 30 percent attributed to actions of the competition to dramatically decrease their selling prices of product made possible by investment in manufacturing technology greatly increasing efficiency, preserving the same quality, but resulting in the need for considerably fewer workers. The decrease in sales had nothing to do with quality or efforts by the BFCC employees who remained dedicated, motivated, and supportive of the company. Notwithstanding the decrease in revenue and the greatly diminished profits, Best retained all his employees throughout 2019 with no decrease in pay, no decrease in hours, and no layoffs.

The bonus system, however, was another matter. For fiscal year 2018 to 2019, the revised bonus system was proposed as follows:

BFCC Bonus System Fiscal Year 2018–19

Salary Rage ($)	Amount of Bonus
40,000 and under	$1,000
40,001–50,000	$1,500
50,001–60,000	$2,000
60,001–70,000	$2,500
70,001 or higher	5% of salary

Reaction from the supervisors and workers was immediate. Supervisors reported that morale was low and falling every day since Best's email to them had been received explaining the situation and presenting the revised bonus system. Efficiency was declining, absenteeism was increasing and productivity was at an all-time low. The word "from the floor" was that employees expected the bonus since they worked even harder this year and that the "global economic situation" was not something they could control and therefore, should not be penalized because of the downturn.

On December 7th BFCC suffered a major fire in one of its warehouses as a result of faulty wiring. Thirty percent of its annual revenues were lost since the warehouse stored a major order being shipped to Europe the next day and sufficient product did not exist to substitute the order. This, coupled with the economic downturn, crippled the company's cash flows and it appeared that layoffs would inevitably result. The more immediate problem was the bonuses: BFCC no longer had the cash flows to pay the bonuses.

Questions

1. You are Martin Best. How would you handle the situation?

2. Critically assess the bonus plan.

3. In your view, and with the full benefit of hindsight, what do you feel would have been a better approach to the bonus system at the outset?

Cardiac Ken

Ken Fraser was the Director of Finance in a major public sector organization. Ken was always uptight, pacing and "vibrating," and transmitted his nervous energy to his staff. He was also inclined to say whatever he felt—without filter—particularly when it came to performance.

Ken's peers and superiors respected his technical ability and his capacity to "get things done on time" (although not always on budget, since his directorate's overtime bill was through the roof). He was also inclined to pick his favourite employees, "favourite" generally applying to those "yes Ken" employees.

Originally from the private sector, Ken joined the public service and moved quickly up the ranks. Never having truly made the mental adjustment necessary to transition from the "bottom line"-oriented, "pressure-cooker" environment of the private sector to the "political efficiency is all that matters" headset of the public sector, Ken was always in a hurry and always pressuring his staff. His approach was steeped in sarcasm and he would publicly berate any of his staff for any perceived "error" or any other shortcoming he felt didn't meet his personal standards. Turnover was not a problem, since the government was going through a major downsizing exercise and in this particular directorate, with the pressure to reduce staff, everyone was lucky to have their job. The alternative was being "laid off," and although any person who was affected had the benefit of six months in which to find another job, the reality was every other organization was going through the same exercise and there was, essentially, no other place to go.

Although Ken's staff consisted of senior and junior financial officers, everyone reported to Ken because "this was the most efficient and effective way of running an organization," according to Ken. There was really no point in suggesting that this might be somewhat unrealistic with forty staff!

At the beginning of the current fiscal year, Human Resources reminded Ken "not to forget the performance appraisals that were due on March 31st." Ken responded to the email by saying "he would be taking the initiative to rethink and redesign his approach to assessing the performance of his staff." What he didn't say to HR was that he viewed the entire appraisal process as a complete "BS waste of time" since with the unionized employees he couldn't fire "the lazy, useless ones anyway," so he needed to design a quick way to comply with meeting the demands of "those idiots in Personnel."

Ken was an accountant and loved numbers. Everything, according to Ken, was about numbers. It came as no surprise when Ken developed a Graphic Rating Scale Appraisal that reflected everything he felt was important to satisfy his expectations. Moreover, it would take no time at all to complete and the same work of art could be applied to every member of his staff. His approach was to fill in the GRS as he saw things, and send them to "that perpetual pain in the.... Personnel Director, Jean-Guy Laflamme" as he completed them, "just like a perpetual inventory system," and send a copy to the employee being rated, follow which, his work on performance appraisals was done! How incredibly efficient and how superior to "that other BS appraisal instrument, with all the silly narratives and nonsense requirements."

Ken's GRS is found below; for his staff member Brenda Daily (*not a* favourite):

Finance Directorate Performance Appraisal Sheet
Period: 1st April 2018–31st March 2019
Brenda Daily

Performance Factor	Performance Rating		
	Completely Unsatisfactory	Completely Satisfactory	Completely Superior
Quality of Work: Timely, Accurate, Complete	X		
Quantity of Work: Volume of Work is the Same as Others in the Unit	X		
Technical Ability: The Ability to Perform the Technical Aspects of the Job Independently	X		
Dependability: Shows up on Time and Works Late; doesn't Complain	X		

Overall Rating:

Unsatisfafctory X

Satisfactory

Superior

This "performance appraisal" was attached to the following email message to the Director of Human Resources, Jean-Guy Laflamme:

Dear Guy,

Please find attached the appraisal for Brenda Daily. She's not the sharpest knife in the drawer! I know you will be very pleased with the streamlining of the appraisal system I am now using. This might be great for the hole (sic) department during these busy times! More of these to follow. Ton ami, Ken

Jean-Guy stared at the screen dumbfounded and muttered out-loud to himself, "Cardiac Ken est-il fou? Ce n'est pas une évaluation de performance! Il ne peut pas être sérieux, bien que ce soit l'idiot Ken qui écrit." Jean-Guy was particularly upset, more than he usually was when he received messages from Ken.

He then forwarded Ken's message and attachment to his boss, the Assistant Deputy Minister of Human Resources, Lucien Peltier. In his message Jean-Guy expressed his concerns ("...*regardez la nouvelle initiative de ce crétin!*"), and recommended that someone from the Peltier's office should discuss the failings of this approach ("...*cela ne pouvait être écrit que par le plus stupide...*") with Ken and help him develop a better approach, if he seriously wants to change the appraisal system for his directorate. Jean-Guy could not bring himself to acknowledge this "*approche absurde de l'évaluation de la performance.*" He ended with a personal note to Lucien:

P.S. Lucien: Si nous cherchons des personnes à libérer, Ken a mon vote!

Required

The Assistant Deputy Minister has forwarded Jean-Guy's message and attachment to you, as his Senior HR Policy Advisor, with instructions "to take care of this mess."

Sunsilva Corporation

In 2019 the Sunsilva Corporation was looking to recruit five new managers for its newest division. A famous consultant, Richmond Hilltop was retained to develop a testing methodology that would ensure candidates could meet the requirements of the position.

The management positions required persons who were experienced, technically competent, excellent communicators, culturally sensitive, with exceptional interpersonal skills. Although designing tests was not Hilltop's specialty, he nonetheless devised a two-hour long test to measure these several traits. Before applying it, he thought it best to have it evaluated by an expert from the local university, Dr. Philomen Smart.

After "testing the test," Smart noted the following:

- The test did not measure two of the most important traits related to the successful performance of the job;

- There was no notable relationship between certain of the test results and the candidate's probable performance.

Smart had other concerns and suggested to Hilltop that he consider using predictive and concurrent validity approaches in refining the test.

Required

1. Discuss what is meant by Smart's observations.

2. Describe how you would use predictive and concurrent approaches to validate Hilltop's test.

Antonio Cerveza and Cerveza Custom Jewellery Inc.

Antonio (Short Tony) Cerveza was a certified gemologist and a highly skilled and internationally renowned designer and manufacturer of custom made costume jewellery. For years Antonio had worked in the United States but recently he became interested in a number of uniquely Canadian gems—the *Sudbury Opal* and the *Thompson Glacier diamond*. Both of these gems were only available in Canada in their raw and unworked form and prevailing Canadian government regulation only permitted export after the raw gems had been finished into gemstones. So if Antonio was to venture into jewellery design using these particular Canadian gemstones, he would be unable to do so from his manufacturing facility in New York.

Antonio's Uncle Carlos was in the warehouse business in Ottawa, Canada, and suggested to his nephew Short Tony that he should seriously consider establishing a jewellery manufacturing facility at one of Carlos' vacant warehouse facilities. In addition to the inexpensive rent that Uncle Carlos would charge and a favourable currency exchange, Carlos advised Short Tony that Ottawa had a good supply of trained gemologists and a relatively affluent population that would be willing customers for custom-designed jewellery pieces that featured Sudbury Opals and Thompson Glacier diamonds. Moreover, being close to the seat of government would make it possible for Short

Tony to develop important contacts that could assist him in developing his export plan for his products.

After a number of emails, meetings, and smart phone text conversations, Short Tony decided to open up a jewellery manufacturing facility in Ottawa. Within a few months he had retrofitted one of the vacant warehouses, purchased all the necessary equipment and was ready to start hiring staff.

In response to a vigorous advertisement campaign both in the local newspapers and through the Internet, over eighty persons applied for forty-five positions. Of the forty-five positions, two were management positions, ten were for certified gemologists who would design innovative jewellery products, and the remainder were hourly-paid positions responsible for operating the machinery that produced the final jewellery products. Short Tony took pride in his ability to hire, among the forty-five successful applicants, a strong representation of women and visible minorities. He also took considerable pride in his business savvy—similar to his approach in New York, he paid his hourly workers at the prevailing minimum wage in Ontario and offered a "bare bones" benefit package to all his employees that met only the minimum legal requirements. His workers were expected to work eight-hour days and forty-hour weeks to a maximum of forty-eight hours per week, and would be paid overtime at one and a half times the regular pay on any number of hours that exceeded forty hours per week. One of his new recruits was designated the company safety officer whose duty was to ensure that everything was running within the provision of the code.

In his first year of operations Short Tony experienced much success. It appeared that Uncle Carlos had been right. Short Tony's domestic market was stronger than expected and he had been able to make significant inroads into several elite target export markets in the United States, England, Germany, and France where the demand for his exquisite designs using the increasingly famous Sudbury Opals and Thompson Glacier diamonds grew steadily.

His staff turnover was surprisingly low and during the course of his first year he expanded his operations and hired an additional twenty staff. One of these more recent hires was Daniel Monette. Daniel joined Cerveza Custom Jewellery as a machine operator after having spent thirty years as machinist in the automobile industry. He had always been interested in jewellery and took this job more as a hobby that as a serious source of income. But Monette's personal financial position was not typical of the other workers and during the few months he had worked for Short Tony he noticed that many of the workers were complaining about the relatively low wages, no pay raises for a year, and meagre benefits. He also was aware of the outrageous mark-ups on jewellery and putting two and two together came to the conclusion that Short Tony could easily afford to pay his workers considerably more than minimum wage.

One morning Monette raised the matter directly with Tony suggesting that Tony should consider rewarding his workers with a pay raise. Tony's reaction was instantaneous—the answer was no.

Several days later while bowling in a house league in which many of the jewellery workers were members, Monette brought up the idea of unionizing. Word of this idea circulated through the grapevine quickly, and the following weekend forty-five workers met at Monette's place to learn more about unionization and how it could help. With the help of email three weeks later Monette applied to the Ontario Labour Relations Board for certification of the Union of Jewellery Workers (UJW) as the official bargaining unit of Cerveza Custom Jewellery.

Short Tony was particularly annoyed when he heard about the movement to establish a union. Previous attempts to form a union in New York were easily thwarted, and he thought that this movement would go nowhere. But when the Ontario Labour Relations Board certified the UJW, Short Tony knew that he would be playing in a bit different game.

Three months into his second year of operation, Monette and three other representatives chosen from the sixty members of the UJW officially met with Short Tony to discuss how labour practices and benefits could be improved. Monette told Tony that in addition to the members from Cerveza Custom Jewellery, the new union was receiving and accepting applications from workers in the jewellery business and gemologists from across the city and he predicted that within twelve months it would be impossible to hire nonunionized workers.

Monette laid out the union demands:

- A collective agreement contract that covered a three-year period that called for:
  - An immediate increase in wages of 20 percent, plus an increment of 5 percent per year over the next two years;
  - An immediate decrease in working hours from forty hours per week to thirty-five hours per week;
  - An immediate increase to the amount paid for overtime—from one and one half times the hourly rate to two times the hourly rate on any number of hours over thirty-five hours per week;
  - Paid medical and dental;
  - Paid private pension contributions;
  - Veto power over the promotion of managerial personnel.

Short Tony, expecting that the union would make certain demands (which is why he never wanted the formation of a union in any of his companies) made the following managerial offer:

- A collective agreement contract that covered a three-year period that called for:
  - An immediate increase of 2 percent being the rate of inflation contained in government reports, plus increments equal to the prevailing adjustments in the consumer price index over the next two years;
  - No decrease in working hours;
  - No increase to the overtime rate;
  - An agreement to look into the possibility of a cost-shared medical and dental plan;
  - No private pension contributions;
  - No veto power of the union over the promotion of managerial personnel.

The meetings continued for the next three months and neither side would make any concessions. In August, the members of the UJW went on strike and Short Tony's operations grinded to a halt. Short Tony and Daniel Monette agreed to obtain the service of Richard (Slick Rick) Fontana, a famous arbitrator who would advise both sides, but as he was not retained as an arbitrator, he could not impose a settlement.

Despite the work of Slick Rick, a settlement was still not possible and by the end of September the union members were wondering whether a strike was the best approach. During July and August, Short Tony had not been idle and had established a new jewellery manufacturing facility in Gatineau, Quebec, that had become operational in mid-September.

On October, Monette indicated to Short Tony that the union members were ready to return to work and to reopen negotiations, but Short Tony refused. A week later he closed the Ottawa manufacturing facility.

Required

Analyze this case from a labour relations point of view.

Marketing Cases

Marketing cases can cover a range of topics and take a narrow view of a unique concept (such as, for example, marketing ethics, social media) or a broader view (such as, the development of a strategic marketing plan).

Case Title	General Area of Focus	Page No.
The Abyss	Marketing and social media	171
Bob's Electric Bingo	Developing a strategic marketing plan	174
Molly's Dog Training	Developing a strategic marketing plan	176
Michaelcraft Inc.	Developing a strategic marketing plan	183
Mulligan's Fancy	Branding, labelling, marketing ethics	190
Coca-Cola and Bottled Water	Analyzing marketing strategies on new product launches (secondary research required)	194
Stone Diamond's Automobile Emporium	Developing a strategic marketing plan	195
Willy's Walleye Wiggler	Marketing, promotion, pricing, distribution	198
Horloge de Jacques	Strategic decision-making	204

The Abyss—Marketing and Social Media

In early 2019 the Braydon Corporation (BC) undertook a major research and development effort to develop a cellular telephone offering that was "water resistant." The idea was generated through a brainstorming session with a group of undergraduate marketing students. The product was labelled the *"abyss."*

The market division at BC decided to focus on offering this product through social media. They decided to offer their product through

Facebook, YouTube, and a specially created blog. They further created a mobile application that would allow customers to purchase their product on line.

One such customer was William Wetsuit (aka Willy the Scuba Pro) who purchased the product for its capacity to take excellent pictures at depths where the water pressure was significant, but also where light was greatly diminished. Willy always believed that cell phones took excellent pictures and would be much lighter than the typical under-water cameras and was perpetually "surfing the web" in search of such a product and the abyss was the only product of its type on offer. Willy happily parted with the $1,800 for his abyss, and while he was not concerned with the risks associated with the abyss' performance, he was concerned that his dive buddies might think he paid too much.

On the day of his first dive to test his abyss Willy's dive buddy Jimmy Taylor remarked that "the abyss was a largely unproven, overpriced product" and that "it really did not suit Willy" as it conveyed that Willy was financially very well-off which was not the case.

After the dive, Willy reviewed the several photos he had taken at 130 feet, and while they were reasonably good, he felt they did not live up to the quality he expected given the money he had paid for the abyss. He planned to contact the BC to see if he could return the product.

1. Willy's reaction to the pictures taken with his abyss after his dive reflects:
    a. An external locus of control
    b. Decision heuristics
    c. Need recognition
    d. Post-purchase dissonance

2. When the Braydon Corporation used Facebook, the company was using which one of the following categories of social media?

   a. Social network sites

   b. Media-sharing sites

   c. Thought-sharing sites

   d. None of the above

3. When the Braydon Corporation used You-Tube, the company was using which one of the following categories of social media?

   a. Social network sites

   b. Media-sharing sites

   c. Thought-sharing sites

   d. None of the above

4. When the Braydon Corporation used their specially developed blog, the company was using which one of the following categories of social media?

   a. Social network sites

   b. Media-sharing sites

   c. Thought-sharing sites

   d. None of the above

5. Willy's concern that his dive buddies might think he paid too much for his abyss best describes:

   a. Financial risk

   b. Psychological risks

   c. Social risks

   d. Physiological risks

Bob's Electric Bingo

Bob Richards had recently graduated from a major North American business school and was contemplating his next career move. Having been a COOP student, combining work periods for credit with his formal studies, Bob knew his interests lay in running his own business. His courses in entrepreneurship helped him realize where his true passion lay, and his major in finance would work well.

While reading the local news online one morning a particular article caught his attention. Old Barney Gates was retiring and closing down the town's bingo hall that had served the small town of Morphster, growing population of 250,000 and home to a tire manufacturing plant and a medicinal marihuana pharmaceutical company, for the last forty years. Decreasing participation due to an aging population demographic and the online gambling opportunities that now competed for his younger clients, old Barney had had enough and at eighty-five years old, lacked both the stamina and the interest to see through any change that could sustain his business. He was going to retire, but a large part of his freedom ninety-five "retirement plan" was the sale of the land and building upon which *Barney's Bingo Basics* stood.

Bob was intrigued with the prospect of innovating a simple concept and differentiating it from similar forms of "entertainment." As well, the opportunity to establish his own bingo offering would meet his needs to be an independent "businessman" and not work for someone else. He decided to speak with Barney Gates.

Following a (very) long meeting at which Barney told Bob the history of Morphster (which Bob already knew, being born and raised there), the history of *Barney's Bingo Basics*, and information on almost everyone, alive or dead, who patronized Barney's establishment, Barney agreed to sell everything to Bob for $300,000. "Everything" included the building (an old converted pool hall with thirty rooms that could be rented out) that could house hundred people, all furniture, signage, and the right of access to the nearby beach on the shores of Lake Morphster—an area used frequently by "bingo-goers." Barney had a recent bank appraisal that valued "everything" at $485,000 to emphasize what a good deal Bob was getting.

Bob also knew that the population of Morphster, while consisting of about 35 percent of persons over the age of seventy, also consisted of 60 percent "millennials." Bob's vision is to lever the millennial's reliance on all things electronic and offer the unique "electric bingo experience." This would include online bingo through an exclusive telephone "ap," but operated in such a way as to require customers to be physically present at the bingo hall to benefit from, not only the bingo games, but also the social aspects including a full bar service, and water sports on Lake Morphster (sailing, kayaking, seadooing).

In thirty minutes, Bob had sketched out a marketing plan, but recognizing his own limitations having not studied marketing, he called an old classmate who was a marketing major. The classmate advised him to take time to develop a strategic marketing plan, and to include things like developing a sustainable competitive advantage, marketing research, consumer decision-making, segmenting, targeting and positioning, and service marketing. Better yet, the classmate strongly recommended that Bob hire a marketing consultant to develop the plan for him, before he bought anything from old Barney.

Bob ended the conversation and thought about all the things that needed to be considered. He also realized that he would need to borrow at least $200,000 of the $300,000 to purchase the business from

Barney. In the end, Bob decided to take his classmate's advice and hire a marketing consultant.

Required

You are the marketing consultant. Prepare a strategic marketing plan for Bob.

Molly's Dog Training

The Key Immediate Marketing Challenge

To create a sustainable competitive advantage for Molly's Dog Training through the expansion of its core business of traditional classroom offerings, increasing instructional offerings in canine behaviour, specialty training and consultations, and day-care offerings.

Company Profile

Owners and Managers

Molly Jones began her professional life as a day-care teacher for pre-school children in 1982. She began instructing dog obedience classes part-time evenings and weekends as a hobby, and founded Molly's Dog Training School in Ottawa in 2004.

Molly's credentials are impressive. Molly is a member of the Canadian Association of Professional Pet Dog Trainers, the Canadian Dog Trainers Association, and the International Positive Dog Training Association. She has attended numerous seminars and taken numerous courses over the years to gain an in-depth understanding and knowledge of the nature of dogs and animal behaviour, and to improve her skills. She has shared this knowledge through the delivery of her courses, as well as having presented at many seminars all over the world. She has also served on the Board of Directors for Therapeutic Paws of Canada, and a number of local a rescue organizations.

Molly is well regarded in the community, and is known for her methods for addressing the needs of dogs with obedience and behavioural issues. She has written several books on the subject of dog training, and maintains a Blog and social media presence to ensure that she remains current and in touch with the dog trainer community and her followers.

Millicent Parker completed Molly's Dog Trainer Program in 2015, and has been instructing and assisting classes under Molly's guidance. Prior to her involvement in Molly's, Millicent worked for a well-known home building supply chain in a middle management position.

Millicent undertakes the majority of the administrative functions at Molly's Dog Training, as well as instructional duties.

Current Business Philosophy and Direction

The dog training facility has always been focused on enabling the integration of a healthy, well-mannered dog into a household, and minimizing conflicts through education about canine behaviour. The school's ultimate goal is to intensify the strong bond between owner and pet. All classes at Molly's are specifically designed to help dog owners teach their dogs to respond reliably to a variety of commands as well as to provide better understanding of canine development and appropriate social behaviour.

The school's training techniques are based on learning theory and stress **reward-based training methods** whereby the dog is set up to succeed and then rewarded for performing the appropriately. Rewards may be in the form of a food, favourite toy, or verbal praise. This type of training is enjoyable for the dog and positively enhances the relationship between the dog and handler. Reward-based training is the most humane and effective way of training all types of animals.

Business Lines

Molly's Dog Training offers the following:

- **Dog Training Classes** including: Puppy, Basic, Intermediate, and Advanced Levels. As well as some specialized training programs including: Freestyle, Agility, and Scenting classes;

- **Private Training** sessions, including general obedience and behaviour assessments;

- **Doggy Day Care** Monday through Fridays from 7 A.M. to 6 P.M.;

- Seminars and Workshops conducted by Molly, and guest speakers on a wide variety of topics concerning general training, identifying, and resolving issues concerning inappropriate behaviours, nutrition, and other areas of physical well-being concerning dogs such as physio, acupuncture, and chiropractic care;

- **The Dog Trainer Program** is a one-year offering that covers the latest information concerning canine physical, cognitive, and emotional capabilities. The program provides for intensive practical experience to reinforce the academic component, and graduates have access to the continued support of Molly's in their chosen field of interest whether it be instructor, dog walker, day care/boarding, rescue work, private instruction, or general interest.

Dog training classes are currently offered on weekday evenings, Monday through Thursday, and on weekends throughout the day. Puppy and

Basic training classes are the 'bread-and-butter" classes. Other more advanced and specialty classes are offered according to demand.

The behaviour aspect of specialty training has been built over time. Group classes are geared toward inappropriate aggressive behaviour directed either toward humans or other animals and other dogs in particular. While there are other schools that now offer this type of training, it has been a major focus and offering of this school since Molly's was established in Ottawa.

Day care is currently offered five days a week with a maximum of five dogs to one trainer. Molly's day care is staffed with a minimum of two trainers at any given time. Generally, competitor day care centres take in twenty dogs per trainer and offer a lower fee; however Molly's does not feel that dogs get adequate attention with the higher trainer\ dog ratio.

Molly's Dog Training has six instructors who are paid at the prevailing minimum wage.

Some Metrics

Molly's has a high return rate of previous clients. A major source of clientele referrals come from veterinarians, breeders, and of course happy clients. A small sample of data gathered through website registration "How did you find us?" reflects the following:

- Forty referred by former clients;
- Eighty former clients;
- Fifty referred by a veterinarian;
- One hundred through the website;
- Thirty-five through Facebook.

Molly's also has excellent relationships with a number of area rescue organizations that refer clients. The current client database contains over 1,900 clients.

The Competition

Molly's Dog Training has been in the current location for fifteen years. The current lease expires in December 2020. The training centre is in close proximity to several Pet Smart locations and several other dog training schools in the Ottawa area.

These competitors may provide many of the same classes but may be limited in their knowledge around specific canine behaviours, or specialize in specific training such as Agility and Fitness classes for dogs, Scenting and Tracking, canine sports such as Flyball and Agility, or day care and grooming.

Other Training Schools offer services to address problems dog owners might have like using physical punishment and suppressive methods, including punishment and negative reinforcement, that Molly's feels are inappropriate and may damage the dog/owner relationship.

Financial information is provided below.

Required

Develop a formal comprehensive strategic marketing plan for Molly's Dog Training that has, as its strategic and operational goals:

- expand the core business through traditional classroom offerings;
- increase instructional offerings in canine behaviour;
- increase offerings of specialty training and consultations, and
- increase day care offerings.

Molly's Dog Training	
Income Statement 01/01/2015 to 12/31/2015	
REVENUE	
Class Revenue	**Total**
Class - Puppy	$ 20,190.00
Class - Basic	$ 22,845.00
Class - Intermediate Obedience	$ 7,512.00
Class - Advanced Obedience	$ 4,022.00
Class - Agility	$ 3,009.00
Class - Behaviour Workshops	$ 8,175.00
Class - Free Style	$ 1,280.00
Class - Leash walking workshop	$ 870.00
Class - Mini Workshops	$ 4,244.00
Class - Off Leash workshop	$ 140.00
Class - Rally-O	$ 406.00
Class - Rescues	$ 266.00
Class - Seminars	$ 7,602.00
Class - Welcome Your New Puppy workshop	$ 400.00
Class Refunds	−$ 1,214.00
Dog Trainer Program	$ 18,000.00
Net Class Revenue	**$ 97,747.00**
Service Revenue	
Seminars	$ 8,218.35
Private Training	$ 10,730.92
Day Care	$ 15,979.19
Total Service Revenue	**$ 34,928.46**
Other Revenue	
Product Sales	$ 604.22
Hall Rental	$ 160.00
Interest Revenue	$ 41.50
Miscellaneous Revenue	$ 454.85
Total Other Revenue	**$ 1,260.57**
TOTAL REVENUE	**$ 133,936.03**

Molly's Dog Training		
Income Statement 01/01/2015 to 12/31/2015		
EXPENSE		
Salaries and Wages		
Trainers - Classes	$	6,377.71
Attendants - Day Care	$	11,284.56
Guest Speakers	$	457.65
Total Salaries and Wages Expense	**$**	**18,119.92**
General and Administrative Expenses		
Accounting and Legal	$	317.95
Advertising and Promotions	$	275.38
Business Fees and Licenses	$	347.40
Computer Expenses	$	114.11
Event Expenses/Refreshments	$	941.64
Insurance	$	1,663.26
Interest and Bank Charges	$	2,534.40
Memberships and Dues	$	227.52
Office Expense	$	2,132.33
Product Purchases	$	406.76
Rent	$	37,575.60
Seminar Expenses	$	4,815.50
Telephone	$	2,319.28
Training Hall Expenses	$	1,132.42
Travel and Entertainment	$	295.52
Utilities	$	3,346.73
Cleaning Supplies	$	152.84
Debit Card Commissions	$	10.80
Paypal Commissions	$	858.15
Visa Commissions	$	1,551.39
MasterCard Commissions	$	914.44
Other Credit Card Commissions	$	72.41
Total Credit Card Commissions	$	3,407.19
Total General and Admin. Expenses	**$**	**65,413.02**
TOTAL EXPENSE	**$**	**83,532.94**
NET INCOME	**$**	**50,403.09**

Michaelcraft Inc.

Michaelcraft Inc. is an Ottawa-based, privately owned company that provides:

- Custom-designed kitchens;
- Custom remodels and renovations for kitchens, bathrooms, and basements;
- Accessible remodelling and renovations for people with mobility challenges.

The Key Immediate Marketing Challenge

Expansion into the "accessibility renovation/remodel" market.

Business Strategy

Michaelcraft's current focus is mid-market kitchen, bathroom and basement design, remodelling and renovations. Kitchens or bathrooms dominate the majority of the work. About 60 percent of basement renovations include a basement bathroom.

Michaelcraft undertakes only complete remodelling projects, referred to as a *"gut and re-do,"* the company does not undertake partial renovations or "fixture-only" renovations. The company has its own in-house, full-time designer.

Only selected subcontractors are used, and only in specific areas of specialization, such as structural engineering, drafting, and electrical.

Additional Information

Market

Michaelcraft operates predominantly in the areas that have homes aged twenty-five year plus. The idea being that a kitchen and bathroom have lifespans of approximately twenty years and need updating accordingly.

Kitchens

Michaelcraft specializes in custom IKEA kitchens. Beginning with IKEA's system, Michaelcraft will add and/or modify cabinets to suit the style the client desires. IKEA cabinets are always in stock, so there is no lead-time issue as with custom cabinetry. (Note: custom cabinets can involve a lead time of eight weeks or more; Michaelcraft feels this is too long for a customer to wait for their new kitchen.)

The average price for a kitchen remodel is $40,000 and takes four weeks on average to complete.

Bathrooms

Michaelcraft uses good quality fixtures—a major challenge in bathroom renovation/remodelling is finding good quality and reasonable priced vanities.

Bathroom projects are priced from the low $20,000's for a three-piece main en suite, to the mid $30,000's for a four-piece main bath.

Basements

Michaelcraft specializes in *warm* basements, incorporating plenty of insulation, Dricore subflooring, and generous amounts of forced air or supplemental electrical heat.

Basement renovations are priced at $40,000+ and require four weeks or more to complete. In terms of age of the home, basement renovations can occur during anytime in the lifespan of house. However, the new-development-basement is not a market that Michaelcraft has been able to penetrate.

Key Cost

By far, the largest component of Michaelcraft costs is labour. The ratio of labour to materials is now greater than 2.5:1.

Territory

Michaelcraft operates on the Ontario side of the Ottawa River from Carleton Place to Embrun (West to East) and from the Ottawa River to Kemptville (North to South).

Company Philosophy

Michaelcraft believes that it has a responsibility to ensure that the customers' hard-earned money is spent wisely and will increase the value of the customer's home as well as bring satisfaction to the customer for years to come. The President is available twenty-four hours a day, seven days a week, 365 days a year to all his clients.

> *"If your toilet backs up at 2:00 AM and you call me, I will get out of bed and get right over to your house and fix it. However, I really don't want to get out of bed, so if we install a good quality toilet correctly, it should not backup."*
>
> —*Philip Michaels, Michaelcraft Inc.*

Michaelcraft believes that good quality does not mean expensive—it means "good quality" and value for the money spent and the company spends considerable time researching existing and new products.

If a product does not meet Michaelcraft's five-year product warranty requirement, the company will not sell it.

Quality and Attention to Detail

Michaelcraft offers a five-year, no-questions-asked warranty on all its work and is proud of its A+ rating with the Better Business Bureau (BBB), and its five-star rating with HOUZZ http://www.houzz.com/, a web-based source for all things related to homes. Michaelcraft's goal is to maintain those ratings and the company will do whatever it takes to make certain its customers continue to provide that rating.

The Michaelcraft team takes on only one project at a time to avoid stretching resources too thin, and focuses on efficiency in all their projects.

> *"We are quite efficient on what we do. (This is an ever evolving process based on experiences and project completion feedback). Our view is that if we can eliminate or reduce the time it takes to do tasks, WITHOUT CUTTING CORNERS that will allow us more time to spend on the finishing touches.*
>
> *For example all our tools are on carts with wheels. Each craftsperson has a designated spot for each tool-think of it like a surgeon always know where their scalpel or clamp is located on the tray that hold all the surgical instruments. I adapted the idea while watching a show on how BMW's were built. Each craftsman had all their tools handy so they could concentrate on the car rather than getting up to search for the tool that she/he needs."*
>
> *—Philip Michaels, Michaelcraft Inc.*

Michaelcraft is concerned with neatness and works hard to minimize the inevitable clutter associated with renovations. All work areas are covered with sheets of masonite to protect floors, and all walkways are covered with rubber walking mats. The entire work area and walkways are vacuumed each night using a HEPA (High Efficiency Particulate Air) filter equipped vacuum.

Owner-Perceived Challenges

Philip Michaels has identified the following key challenges:

- **Getting to the Next Stage (i.e., growing from a small group to a larger group)**

  Where completing *several* single projects with dedicated teams *completing* each project before moving onto the next is a mandatory requirement.

- **Identifying New Markets**

  Michaelcraft is in the early stages of expanding into "aging in place" and "accessible" bathrooms and kitchens.

- **Staffing**

  Finding and retaining highly skilled labour.

- **Differentiation and "Being a Small Fish in a Big Pond"**

  There are a number of large renovation companies in the business, as well as a plethora of smaller ones.

- **Financing**

  Growth into new markets will require investment.

- **Increasing Sales Staff**

  The Philip Michaels is currently the sole salesperson.

Michaelcraft has also identified the following perceived competitive advantages:

- **Huge Web Presence**

  State-of-the-art website which is continuously updated by a full-time web/social media staff member and dedicated programmers located in India.

- **Management and Financial Expertise**

  The president is a qualified CA, CPA.

- **Adaptability**

  Michaelcraft is very quick to respond to queries.

- **Ahead of the Curve**

  Relative to other construction and renovation companies.

Required

Given the above description of Michaelcraft, you are required to conduct background research into the home renovation industry in general, and the area of "accessibility renovations" more specifically, including, among other things:

- Who are Michaelcraft's key competitors in the area of accessibility renovations?

- What is the competition's competitive advantage?

In developing a picture of the external environment in which Michaelcraft is operating, you will also research the population demographics of the territory in which Michaelcraft operates as articulated above.

With this background in mind, you are required to develop a formal strategic marketing plan for Michaelcraft Inc. that has, as its strategic and operational goals:

1. *to expand into the accessibility renovation market in which renovations are performed to assist those persons with mobility challenges to remain safely in their own homes, and,*

2. *to create a sustainable competitive advantage in this growing area.*

To assist in the development of a strategic marketing plan, you must address the following components:

a. Define the Business Mission and Objectives;

b. Conduct a Situation Analysis (Strengths, Weaknesses, Opportunities, and Threats) as well as an examination of market trends, customer analysis, and competitor analysis. The plan should also assess the opportunities and uncertainties of the marketplace due to changes in cultural, demographic, social, technological, economic, and political forces (CDSTEP) where these apply;

c. Identify and evaluate Opportunities for increasing sales and profits by using STP (segmenting, targeting, and positioning);

d. Implement the Marketing Mix and Allocate Resources—in this assignment you would need to implement the marketing mix— product, price, promotion, and place—on the basis of what you believe the target market will value. Product and value creation, branding decisions; Price and value for money; Place and value delivery; and Promotion and value communication;

e. Evaluation and Control Metrics: How will the company assess whether this plan is successful?

Mulligan's Fancy [18]

Billy Mulligan had been born in Belfast, Ireland and immigrated to Ottawa as a child with his parents. He was raised in Ottawa, worked for several years for the Government of Canada, and during that time obtained an MBA degree with a major in marketing.

Billy had always been of a rather entrepreneurial spirit and had a knack for finding niche markets for the most bizarre products, none of which ever brought him significant financial return. However, Billy was undaunted and continuously looked for the next big opportunity.

As Billy neared the age for early retirement he stumbled upon what he thought was an incredible niche market—a milk product for coffee *"with a wee drab of alcohol"* added *"for a bit of a bite."* Billy reasoned that this would make a fine new product similar to eggnog. Over coffee one morning with three buddies it was decided they would pool their severance pay on retirement and go into business as a private corporation selling this milk-based product to be called *Mulligan's Fancy*. The four would serve as the Board of Directors for Mulligan's Fancy Limited (MFL).

Retirement day came and went and within two months MFL was incorporated as a private corporation under the laws of Canada. After obtaining a dairy processors' license, MFL set up shop in Alberta. Alberta had an interesting history when it came to alcohol [19] but more importantly, one of the founders had a sister who was married to a

---

[18] Case written by Dr. David H J Delcorde, Telfer School of Management, University of Ottawa, 2008. This case was inspired by Tom L. Beauchamp: *Marketing Alcoholic Beverages and Its Impact on Underage Drinkers* in Beauchamp. Tom L. *Case Studies in Business, Society, and Ethics*, 5th ed., Pearson Prentice Hall, 2004. This case is fictitious. Any resemblance to persons, companies, or events is coincidental.

[19] "Alberta Gaming, Liquor and Cannabis Commission", Wikipedia.org, http://en.wikipedia.org/wiki/Alberta_Gaming_and_Liquor_Commission, accessed August 6, 2019.

dairy farmer who could legally supply the milk to MFL. The MFL factory opened in Calgary in complete accordance with the Dairy Industry Act[20]. It also obtained all necessary permits from the Government of Alberta in accordance with the Gaming and Liquor Act[21] to permit it to manufacture its product.

Milk of course was a key ingredient, but the alcohol was also unique: It was manufactured on-site at the MFL factory under the watchful eye of Billy's cousin from Dublin, Willy O'Toole, an experienced distillery expert who distilled the "alcohol" by a rather complicated process—completed, as he explained, by *"using sprouted barley dried in a closed kiln, then mixing it with unmalted barley before grinding it into a gris, lad…"*

Billy always loved marketing so while Willy undertook the distillation and mixing with milk, he focused on labelling—deciding on 250-mL milk cartons that featured the caricature in Figure 4 that he developed himself. Next, he thought up the slogan found in Figure 3. Together Billy thought he had a winning combination and so did his fellow founders.

The final packaging also contained a clear warning: **"Warning: product contains 6.5% alcohol by volume."**

The next two months went by quickly as MFL prepared for its product launch. In the end, *Mulligan's Fancy* was released as essentially a fortified milk product containing 6.5 percent alcohol—and featured as an alternative product to wine coolers. Moreover, many workers in the labour trade used it as an additive to their coffee—instead of cream or

---

[20] http://www1.agric.gov.ab.ca/$department/deptdocs.nsf/all/rsb10369

[21] "Gaming, Liquor and Cannabis Act", Alberta.ca, http://www.qp.alberta.ca/1266.cfm?page=g01.cfm&leg_type=Acts&isbncln=9780779806713&display=html, accessed August 6, 2019.

"...have a Billy
Blaster before you
take yor leave..."

Figure III Slogan

Figure IV Leprechuan with cup of beer

whole milk. The famous Parisian Chef Piff *de la* Patoff used it on his television cooking show in most of his recipes instead of regular milk—citing the product as "healthy" *"since it contained less than 1% fat."*

One of the unique characteristics of this beverage was that the "manufacturing process" resulted in a drink that was very light tasting and nonfilling—it was therefore possible to drink two or three of these containers without feeling "full." There were, however, other side-effects...

Over the next year sales skyrocketed in Alberta as virtually every retail outlet with a liquor license carried the product. To raise capital for expansion, MFL "went public" becoming publicly listed on the Alberta Stock Exchange. *Mulligan's Fancy* was now even exported by MFL to several American States and to Europe (even Ireland bought some!). Sales of its shares soared and as its popularity spread, unfortunately so did its problems.

In September, after a frosh party at a local college, a young teenager dropped a rock off a bridge over a highway that hit the grill of a passing sixteen-wheel big rig truck. The driver was not injured but was somewhat incensed. Investigators determined that the fourteen year-old teenager had consumed four cartons of *Mulligan's Fancy* purchased from a nearby store. The teenager's father, a noted attorney, asserted that *Mulligan's Fancy* with its "cutesy" leprechaun logo was nothing but "a wolf in sheep's clothing" and designed precisely to lure unsuspecting young kids into drinking alcohol.

The local grassroots public interest group *Citizens for Greater Corporate Responsibility* (CGCR) also became publicly involved in the case and through advocacy advertisements, news interviews, and magazine advertisements caused a great deal of negative publicity for MFL. In response to the uproar, the government of Alberta threatened to revoke MFL's license unless it agreed to a major and immediate relabelling of its product. This, of course, was unacceptable to MFL's lawyers who argued that the leprechaun caricature and logo were intellectual property and part of the appeal that gave the product its unique market niche. Rebranding would cost millions when in fact the responsibility to monitor who purchased the product was up to the retailers. MFL was adamant that its target market was not under-aged drinkers, and sought to undertake a major advocacy campaign directed at the public as well as a lobbying campaign against the government of Alberta's threat to regulate MFL's labelling and branding.

CGCR mounted a web-based public campaign against MFL for refusing to take responsibility for the frosh party incident and refusing to change its labelling "in the best interests of society." The CGCR webpage was frequently monitored by the *Centre for Public Safety (CPS)*, a public interest advocacy group based in the United States. Once the CPS became aware of the frosh party incident, it conducted some research and found a number of "occurrences" in the United States that could be easily linked to Mulligan's Fancy. The CPS brought pressure on Washington—more specifically the Bureau of Alcohol, Tobacco, and Firearms and the Federal Trade Commission to ban the import of this Canadian beverage unless the product labelling was changed to read: *"This is an intoxicating product – use with extreme caution!"* and *"not to be consumed by children."* New York State Senator Simcoe Smithers recently contacted the Canadian ambassador in New York to advise him that in response to public sentiment, Congress was seriously considering imposing a ban on Mulligan's Fancy in the United States. This would be devastating to MFL as the American export market now represented over 50 percent of company sales.

Of course the news media gave considerable coverage to the MFL situation and this coverage was eventually picked up by European news media and politicians of the European Union who called for an investigation into whether any similar incidents in Europe involving either youth or adults could be attributed to the consumption of *Mulligan's Fancy*.

Required

Discuss the ethical implications of the branding, labelling, and selling of Mulligan's Fancy.

Coca-Cola and Bottled Water

In 1999, Coca-Cola entered the lucrative bottled water market with the launch of Dasani in the United States. By 2001 it was America's biggest brand. Coke saw enormous potential in the United Kingdom and in 2003 revealed to industry insiders that it was bringing a new product to the United Kingdom—"The purest water you could buy."

But something went terribly wrong in the company's marketing strategy and in the end withdrew Dasani from the U.K. market suffering enormous financial loss.

In 2014, Coca-Cola reentered the U.K. bottled water market with its launch of Smartwater in the United Kingdom. [http://www.marketingmagazine.co.uk/article/1295543/coke-dips-its-toes-first-uk-bottled-water-launch-dasani-disaster].

After reading this article and undertaking research into the Dasani U.K. experience:

1. Discuss the key marketing strategy differences observed between these two product launches from the same company in the same market;

2. In your view to what extent was globalization driving Coca-Cola's entrance into the United Kingdom? Were cultural differences a factor in the marketing failure of Dasani?

Stone Diamond's Automobile Emporium

Stone Diamond was a successful automobile salesman with over twenty years' experience selling domestic automobiles in London, Ontario. Mr. Diamond always wanted his own automobile dealership but the up-front franchise costs of buying a franchise offered by one of the major automobile manufacturers was prohibitive.

In the spring of 2019, Stone was sitting in donut shop in downtown London and found himself sitting across from Gino Smith, the owner and operator of Gino's Wheels (GW). GW occupied a choice piece of commercial real estate, across the street from the donut shop and had sold used cars from this location for thirty years. Gino was turning seventy this year, and Stone wanted to wish him a happy birthday. Gino knew Stone by reputation and had spent the last ten years trying to recruit Stone from the local dealership without success.

Through the course of the conversation Gino indicated that he would like to retire and sell the business. This was music to Stone's ears! The conversation continued for two and a half hours. When it ended, Stone and Gino had reached a sales agreement and with a little help from the bank, Gino, Stone's own savings, and a couple of Stone's wealthy relatives, Stone was ready to become an entrepreneur. On July 1st, 2019, Stone Diamond's Automobile Emporium was born.

While Gino dealt in used cars "of all persuasions," Stone had a different idea. He wanted to deal in used cars, but only *higher-end* imported cars with low mileage, documented service history, exceptionally maintained, with no accident history, and not more than three years old. His goal was to become the premier dealer of premium automobiles in London. He would do this by selling the cleanest, most reliable, and most competitively priced used luxury vehicles and by maintaining a fully functional professionally run service department staffed with the best trained and most experienced technicians.

He hoped that in his first year of operations, he could sell one hundred used luxury vehicles and offer service through the service department to 300 customers. Over the next three years he hoped to increase sales by 50 percent and service department revenues by 80 percent. Ten years from now Stone hoped to be selling 500 cars per year and operate with a customer base of 2,000 customers from across

Southern Ontario. In ten years he wanted to be recognized as *the only place to buy a used luxury vehicle in Southern Ontario.*

Stone Diamond knew from experience the importance of analyzing the internal and external environments. In conducting the analysis for Stone Diamond's Automobile Emporium he realized that many residents of London were driving late model imported luxury automobiles and that there were neither import car dealerships in London nor service garages dedicated to servicing these types of automobiles. He knew as well that he had an excellent business plan and he knew the automobile business very well. He also hired five experienced salespersons as well as a seasoned sales manager, and three service technicians as well as a service manager. All his accounting and finance operations would be handled by a local firm of public accountants on a contract basis. His team was stellar.

Stone put together a plan that set out company priorities and the steps that both the sales and service departments would have to take to meet the strategic objectives that he had set for the company. The shorter range plans concerned with implementing the specific aspects of the company's strategic plans were left to the Service and Sales Managers.

Stone decided that he wanted to focus on one product line—more specifically luxury imported automobiles. Growth of his company would be accomplished through market penetration. He also thought that developing a service department would assist in penetrating a related market, one that could serve customers who purchased an automobile from him and those who needed service on their automobile who might become future customers of the sales department. While he wanted to offer competitive prices on his automobiles, he was more interested in evolving a unique company: a company that would be valued by his customers.

To develop this uniqueness, Stone knew that a certain organizational culture would need to evolve. The "feel" of the culture he perceived was one of professionalism, well-dressed, well-groomed, knowledgeable and articulate staff, an extremely clean and well-organized show room and service department, and a family-feeling to the company where open communication was encouraged, and people were not afraid to experiment with innovative ideas that could lead to a sustainable competitive advantage. Stone wanted to create an atmosphere that was conducive to friendliness and one in which staff members wanted to work and customers wanted to be a part of. Stone intended to reward and promote those members of his staff who understood the culture and worked to maintain it.

Required

Develop a strategic marketing plan for Stone Diamond.

Willy's Walleye Wiggler[22]

During the cold Baie-Comeau winter of 2019, Willy Wintergreen discovered a new hobby—building fishing lures. Willy was a passionate fisherman and while he actively fished many different freshwater species, the walleye (*Stizostedion vitreum*) was his favourite game fish. This fish has a dark green back, golden yellow sides and a white belly. The lower tip of the caudal fin is white, and there is a large black blotch at the rear base of the first dorsal fin. The colour of the walleye is highly variable, depending on habitat, with golden colour characteristics in many populations. Usually they are paler

---

[22] All information on the walleye has been taken from Underwater World, from the website of Fisheries and Oceans Canada, accessed 2006. For further information refer to www.dfo-mpo.gc.ca/zone/underwater_sous_marin/walleye/walleye-dore_e.htm

with less obvious black markings in turbid waters and more strikingly marked in clear waters.

Walleye caught by anglers are usually 0.5 to 1.5 kg in weight and more than three years of age. The present angling record is a walleye taken in Old Hickory Lake, Tennessee, in 1960, which was 104.1 cm long and weighed 11.3 kg. The previous long-standing record was a walleye of 10.1 kg caught near Fort Erie, Ontario, in 1943.

The special layer in the retina of the eye *tapetum lucidum*, being extremely sensitive to bright daylight intensities, restricts feeding to twilight or dark periods. Walleye are tolerant of a great range of environmental situations, but appear to reach greatest abundance in large, shallow, turbid lakes. Large streams or rivers, provided they are deep or turbid enough to provide shelter in daylight, are also preferred habitat of the walleye. They use sunken trees, boulder shoals, weed beds, or thicker layers of ice and snow as a shield from the sun. In clear lakes the walleye often lie in contact with the bottom, seemingly resting. In these lakes, they usually feed from top to bottom at night. In more turbid water they are more active during the day, swimming slowly in schools close to the bottom.

Most walleye are caught by still fishing with live minnows and earthworms as bait or with artificial lures such as spinners, spoons, plugs, and jigs. Drifting and trolling are usually the most effective methods used to seek out schools of moving walleye and the twilight periods of sunset and sunrise are the best times for catching the species.

Willy knew from experience that jigs were considered the universal walleye lure and that spinners and spoons works well however much depended on the clarity of the water. In very clear water the walleye would prefer bait that resembled its natural food but the typical colour of natural food would not work well in turbid water. Generally this fish prefers long, slender yellow lures with brass or gold.

While doing some rather technical research over the winter, Willy built a lure that not only included features preferred by walleye, but also a built-in LCD pulsating yellow light that reflected the lure's yellow/brass colours in turbid waters in such a way that he thought the fish would be unable to resist.

Willy built four such lures and in the early spring of 2019 traveled north with his brother Willard from Baie-Comeau to the Manicouagan reservoir where he experienced unbelievable success in taking walleye with the new lure. This experience made Willy believe that producing this lure commercially could be viable as it would appeal not only to private fishermen, but also to commercial fishermen. Willy knew from his research that Canadian commercial fisheries had been harvesting about 4,000 to 5,000 metric tonnes (t) of walleye annually with a landed value of about $8 million.

Willy decided to commercially develop his new lure that he called *Willy's Walleye Wiggler* and recruited a local retired business professor, Fast Eddy, Ph.D., to help him with the business analysis and other components of the marketing plan.

Fast Eddy suggested that Willy strive to develop *Willy's Walleye Wiggler* as a brand and to register the lure with the Canadian Patent Office. He also suggested that Willy invest significantly in excellent packaging and labelling as well as in targeted promotional activities. Fast Eddy reasoned that in order to get customers to purchase the lures they would have to be made aware of it, become knowledgeable about it and like it.

According to Eddy it would be important for Willy to establish an easily identifiable image of the product in the minds of consumers and suggested that the best strategy would be a push strategy. This strategy would be augmented by an advertising strategy that would include Internet marketing, however instead of developing the advertising strategy himself Willy was advised to use an advertising agency. Fast Eddy also recommended that sales promotions be used and he thought that trade show participation would make a significant contribution to "getting the word out" regarding this new lure.

After registering the lure with the Canadian Patent Office, together they attended tradeshows, developed packaging and labelling prototypes, and developed an advertising strategy. They researched the costs of producing the lure en masse and settled on a manufacturing company in Singapore that could manufacture the lure at the lowest cost. Now Willy had to determine a pricing strategy, a distribution mix, a retailing approach, as well as the best approach to physical distribution and transportation.

Willy retained the services of a famous local marketing consultant, Morgan Swartz to assist in the analysis of pricing and in developing pricing and distribution policies. Mr. Swartz had worked for several major corporations in the marketing domain and could command extremely high consulting per diems, but as a personal friend of professor Fast Eddy and an avid walleye fisherman he agreed to work with Willy in exchange for a few samples of *Willy's Walleye Wiggler*.

In setting pricing objectives it was decided that profit maximization would be the fundamental goal, however Morgan cautioned that charging the highest possible price was not always the best approach. The main objective would be to get market share through a cost-oriented pricing approach. First and foremost, Morgan suggested that

Willy research the competition and determine the "going price" of similar products, recognizing that Willy could command a somewhat higher price because of the added LED feature on the lure. Using the information provided from Singapore, Willy calculated that each lure would cost $4.50 to manufacture. There would be additional variable costs per lure of $2.50, and Morgan suggested that he include some amount for profit, for the purposes of calculation. Willy figured that a profit of $2.00 per lure would be acceptable. The selling price would therefore be $9.00 per lure.

Morgan then suggested that Willy use a breakeven analysis to determine how many units would need to be sold to break even. Although the *Willy's Walleye Wiggler* would be manufactured in Singapore, Willy would still need to maintain a storage facility and office premises in Baie-Comeau that would cost $300,000 per year and because these costs were not dependant on the number of lures sold or manufactured, these costs would have to be paid regardless of volume.

The selling price of $9.00 was well in line with the competition and was very competitively priced, given the nouveau technology that *Willy's Walleye Wiggler* featured. Fast Eddy suggested that a higher price be charged to create the perception of higher quality. Willy wanted to charge a lower price than the competition to create market share. Morgan suggested fixed pricing be the approach used when selling the lures through Willy's new website, and that the selling price be reflected as $8.99 regardless of whether the lures were sold online or through a store. He also recommended the use of trade discounts and quantity discounts.

Willy envisioned selling his lures in three ways: online; through his physical facility in Baie-Comeau; and through large franchised retailers.

Willy thought the best approach to distribution would be from the manufacturer to his storage facility, and then from his storage facility directly to the franchised retailers. He reasoned that because the lures sold either online or on-site in Baie-Comeau involved less cost than those shipped to large franchised retailers, these could be sold at a lower price.

Fast Eddy thought that an intensive distribution approach would be preferred, whereas Morgan argued that a selective distribution approach would be better. Both agreed however that the lures should not be carried by bargain retailers, although perhaps featuring the lure on a shopping television channel would be acceptable.

Moving the lures from Singapore to the consumer was hotly debated by Morgan and Fast Eddy. Fast Eddy argued that the lures should be shipped directly to the large franchised retailers and that shipping them first to Baie-Comeau and then to the retailers was inefficient. Morgan countered that it would be necessary to undertake a quality verification before the lures were sent to the franchised retailers. Fast Eddy suggested that perhaps Willy did not really need warehouse facilities and that if appropriate quality assurance controls were put in place at Singapore he could use a distribution centre or even a hub to distribute the lures. Fast Eddy argued for truck transport and Morgan argued for air transport. Willy favoured containerization from Singapore to Baie-Comeau through a common carrier.

Required

1. Analyze the promotional strategy suggested by Fast Eddy.
2. Analyze the pricing and distribution strategies suggested.

Horloge de Jacques, SA

The son of a Winnipeg jeweller, Jacques Horloge was introduced to jewelry at a very young age. As a toddler he played with jewelry tools and watched his father use the time-honoured techniques of jewelry design as he designed and fabricated spectacular arrays of rings and other articles. As he grew up, Jacques became fascinated with watches and under the guidance of a master watch maker employed by his father, quickly learned the time-honoured trade.

Over the years Jacques developed into a master watch repair person, and after spending a significant period of time in Switzerland apprenticing and eventually becoming certified as a watchmaker his dream was to open his own watch manufacturing facility. Jacques believed that the very best watches came from Switzerland and the most sought after Swiss watches were mechanical. The challenge he had from his Winnipeg location was that in order to manufacture a "Swiss" watch, a Swiss law *"regulating the use of the name 'Swiss' for watches"* specified certain minimum conditions that must be fulfilled before a watch can be labelled "Swiss made."[23]

According to this law, a watch is only considered to be Swiss if its movement is Swiss, its movement is case up in Switzerland, the manufacturer carries out the final inspection in Switzerland, and not less than 60 percent of the manufacturing costs are generated in Switzerland. Even if Jacques was to import Swiss movements and install them into casings in Canada, the best he could do would be to present his watches as containing a "Swiss Movement." Even this would require that the

---

[23] The source of information on 'Swiss' and all the technical discussion on watches given in this case is the Federation of the Swiss Watch Industry FH, accessed on June 20, 2019. For more information, please see www.fhs. swiss/eng/swissmade.html

movement be assembled in Switzerland, inspected by the manufacturer in Switzerland, and that the components of Swiss manufacture account for not less than 50 percent of the total value, excluding the costs of assembly, with not less than 60 percent of the manufacturing costs being generated in Switzerland.

Jacques was a purist and decided that to fulfill his dream he would move to Tenniken, Switzerland and, with the help of some wealthy Winnipeg businesspersons, establish his manufacturing facility, *Horloge de Jacques, SA* (HJSA)—a Manufacture d'horlogerie that would produce the components needed for the manufacture of its wristwatches.

The HJSA business plan was well developed. Jacques wanted to concentrate on manufacturing mechanical watches. This was a complicated procedure made particularly demanding since the quality of wrist watch that Jacques wanted to produce required that all assembly be done by hand.

The traditional mechanical watch is made up of roughly 130 parts assembled in three main parts: the source of energy, the regulating parts, and the display. The typical mechanical watch consists of a barrel/mainspring, a gear train, an escapement, a balance wheel and hairspring, a winding stem and/or an oscillating weight, and a dial train. An automatic watch works on the basis of the principle of terrestrial attraction where a rotor turns and transmits its energy to the spring by means of a mechanism. The system was invented in Switzerland by Abraham-Louis Perrelet in the 18th century.

Jacques' watches would not only be mechanical but also chronometers and feature "jewels" as part of the components. A chronometer is a high precision timepiece for which movement, after considerable and rigorous testing, has received an official timing certificate from an official timing bureau such as, for example, the Swiss Institutes for Official Chronometer Testing (C.O.S.C.). Jewels are synthetic sapphires or rubies which have been drilled and polished to serve as bearings for gears that reduce friction on mechanical parts. His watch cases would feature gold plating of 30 microns in thickness and all his watch crystals would be synthetic sapphire.

Jacques' vision was to produce mechanical watches of the highest quality; on a par with watches made by the highly recognized high-end Swiss watch brands, but instead of developing several types of watches, he would focus on dress watches and market them as entirely "made by hand." His watches would be sold only by authorized retailers.

In making the HJSA wristwatches, several processes would be used. His factory would use raw materials and forge the stainless steel watch cases on site. It would also use raw gold as an input to its gold plating process. The factory would also fabricate virtually all moving watch parts from raw materials, the watch dial, the wristlet, and all packaging. The jewels, lizard leather watch straps used on certain models, and the sapphire crystals would be the only components not made from scratch by the factory, but purchased from Swiss suppliers. The markings on the watch dials would be painted by hand and the entire watch assembled by hand. Following preliminary testing at the factory, the watches would then be sent to the C.O.S.C. for further testing and certification as Chronometers. Once certified the watches would be packaged and sent from Tenniken directly to authorized dealers across the globe.

An enormous advertising campaign was launched to tell the world about the new hand-made, Swiss watches "Horloge de Jacques." The watches were presented as so reliable, they would be unconditionally guaranteed under "normal use" for the life of the original purchaser. Jacques put enormous emphasis on extremely high levels of customer service and demanded this from all his authorized dealers.

The process of building a Horloge de Jacques wristwatch was very involved. The *"forgerie"* was responsible for manufacturing the stainless steel watch cases and gold plating those cases for the 18k gold models, as well as the watch dials. The *"machinerie"* was responsible for manufacturing all mainsprings, gears, escapements, hairsprings, winding stems, oscillating weights and the watch hands. The *"qualite"* was responsible for quality control on all parts, pretesting, measurement confirmations, and assembling the appropriate parts from the *machinerie* and the *forgerie* that matched the specific model requirements in a "watch tray." Each watch tray was uniquely numbered to match the number stamped by the *forgerie* on the inside of the case. This served as an inventory control and formed the basis of determining whether a watch was authentic. Every Horloge de Jacques watch would have its own unique serial number.

The next step in the process was the assembling of the *ebauche* or the movement blank that comprised the main plate, the bridges, the train, the winding and setting mechanisms, and the regulator. Once complete, the watchmaker completed the assembly of the watch, attached the crystal and the wristlet or watch band, and adjusted the timing.

The completed timepiece was then sent back to *"qualite"* where tests were performed to ensure all standards were adhered to and the watch was functioning perfectly. Any watches that did not meet performance standards were disassembled and all its parts discarded. All timepieces that passed the internal *"qualite"* tests were then packaged and sent to the C.O.S.C. for certification. The factory produced ten watches per week—an impressive accomplishment since from start to finish; one watch required not less than sixty days to produce. The number of finished watches rejected by *"qualite"* was only two per year, and of the watches sent to C.O.S.C. not one had been rejected.

The Horloge de Jacques was an impressive timepiece, painstakingly manufactured by hand using only the best components in the world. By the end of 2018, the company was regarded as one of the best watch manufacturers in Switzerland, and had won three awards at Basel. Their wristwatches were regarded as works of art—with a price tag to match! The most *inexpensive* model retailed for US$20,000 and the most expensive model that featured several complications such as moon phase, date, and chronometer sold for US$90,000. Despite the cost, the company could hardly keep up with demand and many authorized retailers had waiting lists for the watches.

Since the production of the first Horloge de Jacques wristwatch in early 2014, the company had produced and sold 1,500 wristwatches at an average retail price of US$45,000 per watch. Authorized retailers around the world were not permitted to sell the watches at discount and on average made a profit of approximately US$5,000 per watch. The total cost to HJSA to produce one watch, including all direct and indirect manufacturing costs, selling and administrative expenses, interest expense, and the costs of capital for plant and equipment was approximately 70 percent of the retail selling price. This translated into 30 percent profit before income taxes and approximately US$20 million over the first four years of operation.

Mechanical to Quartz

While very successful, Jacques was very conscious of the actions of competitors, many of whom were experimenting with a new type of movement—one that ran like a traditional quartz watch but that obtained its energy the same way as in a self-winding mechanical movement—in other words a self-winding watch with quartz precision. Unlike a mechanical watch, a quartz watch consists of a battery, an integrated circuit, oscillating quartz, a trimmer, and a stepping motor. While Jacques much preferred the mechanical watch, he knew that many customers preferred quartz. Quartz watches are extremely accurate because of their high frequency of vibrations (32 kHz) and their daily variation is equivalent to considerably less than one second per day, compared to a mechanical watch, the better versions of which allow a variation of less than ten seconds per day based on oscillation frequencies of between 3 to 4 Hz.

HJSA was configured to manufacture mechanical watches and Jacques was very reluctant to make any significant modifications to the facility that might compromise the quality of his mechanical watches by starting to produce quartz watches. Any Horloge de Jacques quartz watch would need to feature impeccable quality and feature the same warranty and reliability as the mechanical watches.

For Jacques, the starting point before any decisions would be made would be a benchmarking exercise. At the same time he would retain a Swiss consulting company to conduct market research. In many respects this move to quartz represented a new market segment for Jacques since it is unusual for customers of high-end mechanical watches to purchase quartz watches.

As well, Jacques needed to consider which business processes needed to be changed if he decided to manufacture quartz watches. Since his factory was unable to produce the integrated circuits or the oscillating quartz these would have to be supplied by a Swiss supplier. In fact to create this new movement would require considerable collaboration by the supplier since the integrated circuits and oscillating quartzes needed did not currently exist as "on the shelf" products of the supplier, who was the most highly regarded manufacturer of quartz and integrated circuits in Switzerland—and Jacques would deal with no other supplier but the best in the business.

Although the quartz watch would sell for less than the mechanical watch and would cost less to produce, Jacques would be uncompromising on quality and wanted to offer a quartz watch that was in all respects superior to anything offered by competitors. He encouraged input from all employees as well as suppliers regarding suggestions to improve quality. Going hand in hand with uncompromised manufacturing quality would be the best *service* quality in the business—all authorized retailers would be required to visit Tenniken, observe all steps of the production process, and attend a three-day session on customer service.

As Jacques seriously considered implementing the manufacture of a quartz line of watches, he pondered which parts of the existing production process for mechanical watches could be used for the production of quartz watches. His factory would continue to use raw materials and forge the stainless steel watch cases on site. It would also continue the use of raw gold as an input to its gold plating process. The factory would continue to fabricate all moving watch parts from raw materials, the watch dial, the wristlet, and all packaging. However, in addition to the jewels, lizard leather watch straps used on certain models, and the sapphire crystals, the oscillating quartz, and integrated circuit would all be outsourced from Swiss suppliers. The markings on the quartz watch dials would continue to be painted by hand and the entire quartz watch would be assembled by hand.

Compared to the production of his mechanical watches, the building of a quartz watch was simplified to a certain degree. In terms of "departments" within HJSA the *"forgerie"* would remain responsible for manufacturing the stainless steel watch cases and gold plating those cases for the 18k gold models, as well as the watch dials. The *"machinerie"* would produce only the moving parts of the quartz watch. The *"qualite"* would be responsible for quality control on all moving parts, pretesting, measurement confirmations, testing the quartz and integrated circuits, and assembling the appropriate parts from the *machinerie* and the *forgerie* that matched the specific model requirements in a "watch tray." As with the mechanical watches, each watch tray would be uniquely numbered to match the number stamped by the *forgerie* on the inside of the case. This served as an inventory control and formed the basis of determining whether a watch was authentic. As with the mechanical watches, every Horloge de Jacques quartz watch would have its own unique serial number.

The next step in the process would be the assembling of the watch by the watchmaker.

The completed timepiece would then be sent back to *"qualite"* where tests were performed to ensure all standards were adhered to and the watch was functioning perfectly. Any watches that did not meet performance standards were disassembled and all its parts discarded. All timepieces that passed internal quality testing would be packaged and distributed to authorized retailers around the world.

Required

Advise Jacques whether, in your view, he should pursue developing quartz watches. What factors should he consider from a marketing and business perspective?

Accounting, Finance, and Auditing Cases

The Micron Corporation

The Micron Corporation was the end result of a three-person partnership which imported textiles from India. The business became very successful in 2015.

Smith, Webster, and Brandt, the original partners, were all corporate directors in Micron. Annual compensation for each of the three directors was $250,000 plus a bonus of 2 percent of net income. In 2015, net income for the Micron Corporation was $1,450,000, of which $250,000 was provided to each director, and the remainder reinvested into the corporation.

In 2016, net income for the Mutual Corporation was $1,855,000, and the directors felt that it might be prudent to consider expansion. Two options for expansion were considered. The first option was to purchase a nearby warehouse, which could be bought for $850,000. Fit-up costs would be $220,000, annual taxes were $80,000, and operating costs would be $500,000 per year. The warehouse would allow Micron to increase the number of lines of textiles and increase its offerings to Europe and the Middle East. It was expected that net income would increase 12 percent over the 2016 net income under the warehouse purchase option.

The second option was to diversify from textiles into the completely unrelated area of battery recycling. Under this option, the corporation could use an existing vacant building, which they already owned. Fit-up costs were estimated at $685,000, operating costs would be $450,000, and the necessary equipment would cost $800,000. This option would allow the corporation to branch into the lucrative area of post-consumer waste recycling and increase net income over 2016 by seven percent.

The corporation controls inventory on the basis of First-in/First-out and generally holds about $3,000,000 in inventory of textiles at any one time.

In 2017, inflation was a significant factor for all business. For the Micron Corporation, inflation was a menace, because of the effect of rising prices on inventories. The Micron accountant has recommended changing inventory methods from FIFO to LIFO.

Required

1. What impact on net income would a change from FIFO to LIFO have in a period of rising prices?

2. Under this scenario of high inflation, and based on the information provide in the case, which expansion option would you recommend and why?

3. What would be the effect on Micron's Statement of Changes in Financial Position if the method of inventory changed from FIFO to LIFO?

4. If the directors' bonuses were based on a percentage of tax savings, would change from FIFO to LIFO increase or decrease their bonuses?

5. Proponents of the LIFO method claim the method provides a matching of current costs with current revenues, and that it accurately describes the raising of selling prices when replacement costs increase, despite the fact that older merchandise may be in stock at a lower original cost. Do you agree with this assessment? What arguments can be made *against* LIFO?

The Standard Elevator Company

Art Renaud, the credit manager of the Standard Elevator Company (SEC), was a believer in the five Cs of credit. Art thought that a customer's **character, capacity** to pay, **capital** position, **collateral** and the prevailing economic **conditions** were the (only) criteria required to determine a credit risk.

For many years, Art had operated this way, developing what he called a probable loss ratio associated with a customer's class rating. Based on his accumulated statistics, Art developed a table (Table 1 in Annex A), correlating six classes of customer risk with a probable loss ratio expressed as a percentage of sales on credit. Art has determined that all customers rated at Class 4 and above contribute positively to profits. It should be noted that SEC has no retail customers, installing and servicing elevators for its 200 commercial clients.

In 2018, 80 percent of total sales were on credit. Also in 2017, of the same 200 customers, 135 customers were in risk Classes 1, 2, or 3.

Economic recession has caused some companies to slow payments, so they can maximize the use of their cash assets.

It is of particular interest that, of the customers in risk Classes 4 and 5, 30 percent of Class 5 and 50 percent of those in Class 4 have advised Art, in no uncertain terms, that they do not appreciate his efforts to speed trade accounts receivable collections. If SEC cannot display a bit more compassion and understanding in light of the tough economic times, then these customers are prepared to take their business elsewhere. A nearby competitor, Milcroft Elevator Company, is hungry for contracts and willing to at least match the terms of SEC's contracts.

Recently, SEC's Board of Directors expressed concern over the amount of accounts receivable. Art was instructed to reduce the potential bad debts from credit sales to not more than 2 percent of all credit sales, "through whatever means necessary."

In response to this directive, Art has considered reworking his system to base his risk class and loss ratios on a customer's performance, based on credit terms of net thirty days, instead of the current net sixty day policy. The effect of requiring these same credit customers to pay every thirty days instead of every sixty days is reflected in Tables 2 and 3 of Annex A. This modification will require that Art aggressively pursues past due accounts. Under this scenario it is anticipated that all the customers in risk Class 6 will not pay and thus will be considered as Bad Debts.

Required

Advise Art on whether he should implement the new credit terms.

Annex A

Table 1

Standard Elevator Corporation
Risk Class and Probably Loss Ratio in %

Risk Class	Probably Loss Ratio $
1	None
2	1
3	2
4	4
5	6
6	10

Table 2

Standard Elevator Corporation
Credit Customers by Risk Class
As at 31 December 2018
Credit Policy Net 60 Days

Risk Class	No. of Customers	Total Amount Owed ($)
1	10	100,000
2	30	400,000
3	65	660,000
4	60	750,000
5	20	400,000
6	15	190,000
	200	2,500,000

Annex A

Table 3

Standard Elevator Corporation
Credit Customers by Risk Class
As at 31 December 2018
Credit Policy Net 30 Days

Risk Class	No. of Customers	Total Amount Owed ($)
1	10	100,000
2	10	100,000
3	65	800,000
4	70	800,000
5	25	450,000
6	20	250,000
	200	2,500,000

The Bentley Company Ltd.

In 2018, the Comptroller for the Calais Corporation handed down the corporation's operating budget for 2019. In the budget presentation, it was highlighted that the fiscal year 2019 would be the first year of capital rationing.

The company's policy on capital rationing provided limited funds (not to exceed $2,500,000) for fixed-asset expansion in all divisions of the company. Each divisional manager was requested to decrease expansion proposal and submit to the Comptroller only those that maximized the project's Net Present Value (NPV) per dollar of initial cost.

The budget presentation was attached to the Comptroller's email message, along with an explanation of the concept of NPV. The idea was that the present value of the expected net cash flows per year would be calculated by multiplying a "PVIF" factor by the expected annual net cash flow, to arrive at the present value of the cash flow. This present value would be added for each year of expected cash flows for the project; the project's initial cost would be subtracted from this total. The more positive this value was, the more acceptable was the project from an investment viewpoint, since if the NPV of a project is positive, the increase in the value of the firm is greater than the amount of funds needed to finance the investment.

The following PVIF factors were provided in his email message:

Period	10%	12%
1	.909	.893
2	.826	.797
3	.751	.712
4	.683	.636
5	.621	.567
6	.564	.507
7	.513	.452

"Period" referred to the number of years the project would run.

The Comptroller also provided a sample calculation to assist managers in working out the financial details. He considered a three-year project providing net cash flows of $500, $300, and $200 in years 1, 2, and 3, respectively. The cost of financing was 10 percent and the initial cost of the project was $800. The NPV was calculated as follows:

Year	Net Cash Flow	PVIF	PV of Cash Flow ($)
1	500	0.91	$55
2	300	0.83	249
3	200	0.75	150
PV of Inflows			854
Less: Cost			800
Net Present Value			54

Michael Moorehead, Director of Operations, was the last divisional manager to prepare his submission for capital projects. He was considering the following three projects:

1. The purchase of a state-of-the-art loading machine:

2. This machine would have provided cash flows of $30,000, $28,000, $27,000 in years 1, 2, and 3, respectively. The cost of capital was 12 percent and the initial cost of the machine was $60,000.

3. The purchase of a fleet of transport trucks:

4. The fleet would have provided cash flows of $125,000, $115,000, and $110,000 in years 1, 2, and 3, respectively. The cost of capital in this case would be ten percent and the initial cost of the fleet would be $200,000.

5. The purchase of a storage building:

6. The building cost $250,000 and half of it could be rented to another firm, which would make annual payments of $60,000 per year. Bentley would pay mortgage payments of $1,500 per month. Both the mortgage payments and the rent from the tenant would continue for six years. The cost of capital was 12 percent for this project. (Ignore mortgage interest rates and mortgage payout amounts after the fifth year).

7. A preliminary summary of those projects already submitted by other divisions is reflected in the attached Annex A.

Required

Advise Moorehead on the NPV of his three projects, whether all three projects should be submitted to the Comptroller, and of the projects submitted, what his chances will be of having them approved, in light of the capital rationing policy in force for 2019.

Annex A

Bentley Company Limited
Possible Capital Projects 2019

Proposal	Project's Initial Cost ($)	Project's NPV ($)	Ratio of NPV to Project's Cost
Purchase of Lease Space	450,000	125,000	0.28
Installation of New Accounting System	800,000	235,000	0.29
Installation of Conveyor System	675,000	125,000	0.19
Machine Shop Modernization	300,000	15,000	0.05
Purchase of Computerized Inventory System	275,000	45,000	0.16

Roblin Fertilizer Company Ltd.

Roblin Fertilizer Ltd. is a successful manufacturer of lawn chemicals. The lawn chemical industry is on a recent downturn due to economic uncertainty and both domestic and commercial customers having less available funds for aesthetically pleasing lawns. However RFC is doing very well, much better than others in the industry, partly as a result of its aggressive marketing techniques and that salaries are kept low, in favour of a very generous profit-sharing plan. At the same time the company manages costs in a somewhat ruthless way; when profits began to fall last year, the company responded by laying off 10 percent of its employees.

Glenn's Construction and Landscaping Company is a major customer of RFC. Glenn's is owned by Glenn Savoie, the brother of Michael Savoie, President and CEO of RFC. This year, RFC sold a subsidiary, Uptown Gardening Tools (at a loss), to Glenn's Construction and Landscaping Company. The loss was incurred after it was determined that when RFC bought Uptown the year before, its inventory and patents were overvalued.

Despite the loss on the sale of Uptown and a considerably reduced volume of sales, profits in the first six months of this year are only 5 percent less than profits in the same period last year.

Accounting personnel appear competent but largely overworked, partly because of the effects of the downsizing, and partly because all the accounting records and source documents are maintained offsite by Cheryl Savoie, Michael's sister in-law, who is married to Glenn. The firm believes funds that might be used for automation are better used in marketing areas. RFC is highly debt-finance and the company is reluctant to decrease earnings per share by raising capital through the issuing of shares.

Required

You are an auditor retained by the Board of Directors of RFC. This is your firm's first audit of RFC, the past auditors being discharged for some undisclosed reason. Outline your assessment of elements of risk and materiality in this situation, and indicate what you would do before accepting the engagement.

Bob Brass's Bowling Bash (*the Four Bs*)

In early 2017, Robert (Bob) Brass opened Bob Brass's Bowling Bash (affectionately referred to as the *Four Bs*), a multi-lane bowling alley in Saskatoon, Saskatchewan, on land purchased from his uncle, the famous professional bowler Teflon Crass Brass, for $25,000. His buddy told him that this particular piece of land would be worth next to nothing in three years. He contracted with a general contractor to build *The Four Bs* and completed the job at a cost of $90,000 which he financed through a mortgage for the full amount. The building was completed on 1st January, 2018, and was valued on the market on December 31st, 2018 at $120,000. The building was expected to have a useful life of fifteen years and have no residual value.

The *Four Bs* featured leading-edge state of the arts technology whereby bowlers' scores were kept electronically and running averages were kept for individual bowlers and for teams from the various leagues that played almost every evening. The technology cost $10,000 on January 1st, 2018, had a useful life of one year and no residual value. Other equipment was long term with an initial cost on 1st January, 2018 of $50,000. It was expected to have a useful life of five years and a residual value of $5,000.

The *Four Bs* was a full service provider—in addition to providing the bowling alleys, it also provided ancillary and complementary services including, for example, the rental of bowling shoes, bowling lessons, and a fully appointed snack bar and licensed beverage bar.

Years ago Bob took a bookkeeping course and to save money, he did his own accounting and bookkeeping. By the end of 2018, Bob Brass was enjoying considerable success as the financial statements for the *Four Bs* (prepared by Bob, of course) suggest in Tables 1 and 2 below:

Table 1 Bob Brass's Bowling Bash Income Statement

Bob Brass's Bowling Bash Income Statement As at December 31st, 2018		
Revenues (all sources)	$	$190,000
Expenses:		
Cost of Goods Sold	$45,000	
Advertising	10,000	
Salaries	50,000	
Supplies	25,000	
Utilities	10,000	
Miscellaneous	10,000	
Interest	5,000	
Depreciation Expense – Building	6,000	
Depreciation Expense – Equipment	9,000	
Total expenses	$170,000	
Net Income		$20,000

Table 2 Bob Brass's Bowling Bash Balance Sheet

Bob Brass's Boowling Bash Balance Sheet As at December 31st, 2018			
Current Assets:			
Cash		$15,000	
Marketable Securities		5,000	
Accounts Receivable		10,000	
Inventory		30,000	
Land	25,000		
Less: Accumulated Depreciation	10,000*	35,000*	
Buildings		90,000*	
Equipment		50,000*	
Total Assets		$235,000*	
Liabilities:			
Accounts Payable			$18,000
Wages Payable			5,000
Taxes Payable			10,000
Mortgage Payable			85,000
Total Liabilities			118,000
Owner's Equity			
Bob Bass, Capital 1st January, 2018			$72,000
Add: Net Income			20,000
Add: Adjustment to Balance to Assets			25,000*
Bob Bass, Capital 31st December, 2018			117,000*
Total Liabilities and Owner's Equity			
			$235,000*

Bob's nephew Freddy, who studied Accounting at the South Pole Technical University, told his Uncle Bob that "…while the formatting of the income statement was a little *shaky*, based on a cursory review of the source documents, it appears the numbers appearing in the Income Statement were correct." Freddy didn't have time to verify any of the numbers on the Balance Sheet, but quickly put a mark (*) beside each balance sheet account that he thought was incorrect and needed further analysis. He also suggested that Uncle Bob "…hire an accountant to produce a set of *correct* financial statements in good form, and to ensure the correct application of revenue recognition, matching, and full disclosure."

Just before he left, Freddy gave Uncle Bob the sheet of information he had downloaded from the website of the Last Chance Bank of Saskatoon (see Table 3) and suggested that Bob compare the results for the *Four Bs* with this information to provide a better gauge of how his company was actually doing. And as he was driving away with the top down on his 1980 Lebaron convertible (his *decapotable noire* as he referred to it), Freddy yelled at Uncle Bob "…not to forget that he had to pay slimy Teflon Crass Brass for the land in U.S. dollars, and he couldn't quite recall whether the number indicated on the Balance Sheet was in American or Canadian dollars…"

Table 3 Last Chance Bank Financial Ratios

Last Channce Bank Financial ratios for Bowling Alley Entities in Saskatchewan	
Current Ratio	3.50
Debt to Owners Equity Ratio	0.50
Return on Equity	35.0

Bob Brass watched Freddy drive away, but thought it might be best to hire a consultant to make sense of all this.

Required

You are the consultant. Analyze the information provided in this case and advise Bob.

Interactions between Business, Government, and Civil Society

These cases cover a range of areas that exemplify the interaction, dependence, and influence of business, government, and civil society on each other. No management education is complete without an understanding of these important players.

Case Title	General Area of Focus	Page No.
Barclay's Chemical Foundries (BCF) Ltd.	Advocacy advertising	229
Compound Y	Government Regulation and Intellectual Property Rights in the pharmaceutical industry	233
The Rolling Rubber Tire Corporation	Lobbying	235
Universal Silicon Inc.	Public Private Partnership & Civil Society Interest Groups	239
Friends of Canada's Freshwaters	Business and Civil Society	245
Robert Hinton's Janitorial Cleaning Service	Interaction of ethics, lobbying, social capital, culture, regulation	247

Barclay's Chemical Foundries (BCF) Ltd.

Matthew Tankard couldn't believe what he was reading on the Internet. The Coalition for the Protection of the Natural Environment (CPNE) was spearheading a public protest fuelled by recent allegations made by a number of people on a chat group that chemical lawn fertilizers manufactured by BCF Ltd. were seeping into the water table, causing permanent environmental damage. As the CEO of BCF Ltd., Tankard was shocked to learn that BCF Ltd. was the subject of such allegations. His company had a stellar environmental record and had been cited repeatedly by numerous groups as the "benchmark" in ethical conduct, social responsibility, and environmental responsibility. He had never heard of CPNE but a quick search produced an interesting array of details—the most disturbing was the alleged list of supporters that included some prominent politicians, CEOs of some of his competitors, and even some larger non-government organizations.

As Tankard continued reading, he became even more uneasy with what appeared to be a disinformation campaign targeted at BCF Ltd. that suggested CPNE would retain a lobbyist to lobby the Minister of Natural Resources and the Minister of the Environment to effect new regulations to the legislation concerning the manufacture of pesticides and fertilizers which, if successful, would require such a massive change to BCF Ltd.'s current manufacturing process that it was doubtful the company would survive. Even though it appeared that CPNE was neither particularly well funded nor organized, Tankard was still concerned with, given the ease of telecommunications these days, how such a disinformation campaign, although patently untrue, could cause havoc for the company. This was particularly true given his own experience dealing with government—how they always seemed more concerned with caving to these information campaigns "for the good of the people" and completely uninterested in the business sector. The government, according to Tankard, "just didn't get it"—politicians and bureaucrats didn't understand business. Just about the last thing BCF Ltd. in particular and the industry in general needed was for this matter to be referred to some think tank for further study!

Tankard picked up the telephone and dialled the number of Clinton Morseman—a senior partner in the lobbying firm that BCF Ltd. used regularly to, among other things, keep apprised of what the government was up to that could affect his company and the industry. He needed to know two things: (1) why Morseman didn't advise him of this development and (2) what to do about it!

"Clint, this is Matt Tankard at Barclay's," announced Matt when Clinton Morseman came on the line.

"Matt, great to hear from you and I bet you're calling about the CPNE," replied Moresman.

"You mean you know about this group and its recent antics against Barclay's?"

"Yes, but be aware that this Coalition for the Protection of the Natural Environment is a brand new entity and is not only singling out Barclay's but every other successful chemical manufacturer. It's making many claims regarding its supporters, including a well-known international entertainer—who, apparently, has not even heard of this group, according to her publicist."

"Perhaps like the CEOs of Barclay's competitors?" asked Tankard.

"Including you, as a matter of fact," replied Morseman.

"That's ludicrous! I have never …"

"Yes, I know Matt. But these upstart grass roots groups come to light regularly and truly are not doing any favours to the legitimate civil society organizations that bring real issues to the public."

"So what do we do about this?" asked Tankard. "Write the ministers? Mount our own lobby? And what about the competition?"

"Those are some options of course Matt, and I'd be happy to develop a lobbying strategy with your money, of course! But there might be a more effective way—one in which we could combine the efforts of your company and your competitors to set the record straight about the environmental impact of our industry."

"Advocacy advertising?" asked Tankard.

"Precisely," responded Morseman. "This is all about educating the public before the rhetoric causes permanent and expensive damage to the industry. Once we get the advocacy campaign launched, we can make a few calls to Ottawa and set the record straight. Don't worry Matt, this group may have actually done us a favour—all competitors working together for a change on a common cause, something so rare even the government would have to notice and take what we are doing very seriously. There is another action that I would recommend. The National Environmentalist Association (NEA) is listed as a supporter of the CPNE and the industry association that you and all your competitors belong to, has a number of, shall we say, funding arrangements that provide resources to the NEA. I think a call from the NEA to the CPNE could be provoked with some vague messaging around the renewal of NEA funding being in question if the companies had to fund a lobbying effort. Times are tough financially for all of us Matt!"

Tankard began to relax a bit. "I can almost see you smiling Clint. So when do we start?"

"I have started already. I'll stop by later this afternoon and we can discuss the details."

Compound Y

Early in 2018, after several years of work and considerable investment in research and development, researchers at the Venn Pharmaceutical Company (VPC) had completed blind tests using Compound Y on laboratory rats previously induced to develop vestibular schwannomas, malignant primary brain tumours—the usual treatment for which included traditional and stereotactic surgery, radiation therapy, and chemotherapy; all rather uninspiring. In every instance, following a three-week regime of intravenous Compound Y, the inflicted rats made a full recovery. VPC also conducted tests on human tissue samples and had obtained a Health Canada Clinical Trial Authorization. The company was now in phase 2 of its clinical trial process where "Compound Y Therapy" was being administered to 150 patients with the disease and showing the same amazing results, catalyzing VPC into seeking a waiver from phase 3 of the clinical trial process and seeking an immediate New Drug Submission Review in order to fast track Compound Y becoming a Schedule 1 Drug and available to the public. Fast tracking the approval however was not looking promising as Health Canada officials were adamant that the full-phased clinical trials be completed before the new drug submission review would occur. This, they said, was the procedure and in the public's interest. VPC argued that the residual risk involved was more than offset by the potential health benefits. VPC management was also concerned about having their intellectual property "scooped" before they could recover the significant investment in the drug's development. Health Canada also advised VPC that recovering the costs would be a longer-term matter as, even if the drug was eventually approved as a Schedule 1, its costs to the public would be regulated by the Patent Medicine Prices Review Board, and this would involve additional time.

VPC's phase 2 clinical trials progressed without negative incident until May, 2009, when one patient died. The autopsy confirmed the cause of death was heart failure, caused by hardening of the arteries. A second patient died of heart failure in June, 2009 attributed to the same cause. In both cases there was no history of heart disease in either family. By August 2009, eight more patients had died from heart failure and in each case death was attributed to arterial constriction caused by the build-up of plaque. Health Canada moved quickly to revoke Venn's clinical trial authorization, pending additional and robust scientific analysis that would rule out a relationship between rapid plaque formation and Compound Y. Despite the government's action, many patients inflicted with vestibular schwannomas wanted to continue with the clinical trials indicating they would be quite willing to assume the risk. VPC argued that it could use an existing approved treatment to reduce plaque formation that would more than mitigate the risks to patients in the clinical trials. The government argued that this would not be prudent since the cause and effect relationship had not been scientifically established and that the effect of using the plaque reducing medication with the Compound Y was unknown.

Around the time of the interruption of clinical trials, Venn received news from its public relations research department that a Japanese company, Angin-san Corporation was starting human trials with a drug that was very similar to Compound Y. Venn raised the matter with the federal government, arguing that its clinical trials should not only be allowed to proceed but the government should also waive phase 3 of the clinical trial process, as originally requested by Venn. VPC argued that according to the government's own literature, regulation "is intended to promote a fair and competitive market economy" and clearly this delay on the part of the government is compromising VPC's ability to compete. If Japan can bring a similar treatment to the public before Venn, then VPC would lose millions of dollars invested in research and development.

The government argued back that social regulation as it relates to the health and safety of its citizens is more important than any economic argument VPC could offer and that it must protect the public interest and make decisions based on hard evidence. Until the evidence could be provided by VPC it had no intention of authorizing a continuation of phase 2 clinical trials and under no conditions would phase 3 of the clinical trials be waived. The government noted that VPC would have access to the courts if it thought Angin-san Corporation was infringing on its intellectual property rights.

Questions:

1. In your view, is the government correct in its position on this issue? Justify your response.

2. How does this case demonstrate arguments for and against government regulation of business?

The Rolling Rubber Tire Corporation

Gabe Forester was the Vice President of Operations for the Rolling Rubber Tire Corporation (RRTC) based in Toronto, Ontario. RRTC was a Canadian-owned and Canadian-operated manufacturer of automobile and light truck tires. At a time when most tires were being manufactured offshore, RRTC manufactured its own tires in Canada, using old tires, nylon, plastics, and other discarded post-consumer and commercial waste as inputs. The environmentally responsible manufacturing operation was made possible through the application of new technologies that reduced both emissions and the by-products of the manufacturing process to very low levels. The tires resulting from this process met all existing industry standards and were priced within 10 percent of competitive offerings brought in from offshore manufacturing facilities.

At the Monday morning management committee meeting, the senior management team was debriefed by the company's Vice President of Public Relations, Earl Minion, that in the coming weeks, a Member of Parliament would table a Private Members' Bill that would call for the federal government to enact legislation that would raise the minimum performance standards on all tires installed on all vehicles in Canada. The new standards would require, among other things, a 40,000 kilometre manufacturer's warranty requiring the complete replacement of any tire found to be defective for any reason at manufacturer's expense, regardless of the number of kilometres on the tire up to and including 40,000 kilometres, without adjustment for tread wear. Further, all manufacturers would need to submit each tire type to be sold to rigorous government testing that would be conducted by a consumer group in partnership with the federal government, the cost of this testing to be borne by the manufacturers.

This possible legislation was driven by growing concerns expressed by citizens and consumer protection groups to provincial and federal politicians, of diminishing quality, unreasonable replacement costs even when "under warranty" arising from the application of warranty adjustments that reduced the amount of coverage in accordance with tread wear, and an increasing incidence of blow-outs and leakage around the tire bead and tire valve areas.

"Not to worry lads," said Ed O'Malley the company's Comptroller. "One of my neighbours is a senator and I have a buddy who works as a Director for Transport Canada. I'll speak to these folks and they will derail this ridiculous bill."

"You can try that Ed," said Robert Rolling, the company President and Chief Executive Officer, "but what I would like to know is why we are just finding out about this now?"

"Well you know how the government works Bob," replied Earl Minion. "Legislation can come from anywhere and there is typically little consultation. Besides, it's just a private member's bill—nothing to worry about. If it even survives it will be sent to committee and then we can wade into the debate."

Gabe listened quietly to the briefing, silently contemplating what this might mean for the company, how this could happen, *whether* it would happen, and what the company could do about it.

After returning to his office, Gabe Forester called his old friend, Martin Robarto, a retired federal Assistant Deputy Minister to get his take on Earl Minion's debrief.

"So is this real Martin?" asked Gabe.

"It is certainly not unusual for Members of Parliament to table Private Members' Bills, but whether this particular bill would result in legislation is another matter entirely," replied Robarto. "I would think this level of impact on the industry would certainly demand more profile, and its success without such rigor would be unlikely. That said, you need to engage in the debate Gabe. RRTC should be engaging your local MP now, indicating that you've heard about this and highlighting the negative impact this would have on votes in her riding and in other ridings where your industry is strongly represented."

"Martin, they can't just spring this on us! I've heard from Earl that considerable work has been done on the legislation and that there have been consultations—with whom, and when is what I would like to know. No one asked RRTC!"

"There may very well have been consultations Gabe. The failure here is that RRTC was disengaged with some political activities that directly influence your industry and your company. RRTC and every other company must be proactive in monitoring legislation and government activities, ministerial speeches, and other forms of exhortation that could hold hints, frequently not that subtle, of emerging policy direction. This activity is critical and obviously RRTC has not done it."

"So what about O'Malley's Senator neighbour and his Director buddy from transport Canada?" questioned Gabe. "Can they "kill the bill"?

"The private members' bill will be introduced in the House and it is a long journey from the House to the Senate," replied Martin. "As far as the TC Director goes, the probability of a bureaucrat attempting to influence legislation is zero, and even if this director was crazy enough to get involved somehow, we both know where the his or her position falls in the bureaucratic food chain!"

"What about Earl's pessimism surrounding the success of private members' bills?" asked Gabe. "Any salience to this?"

"Well in my view private members' bills are enjoying a bit more success these days than in previous Parliaments. Regardless, a bill is a bill, and any bill can result in legislation so you should take this seriously. And you can tell Earl that he is dead wrong about consultation. The government has made consultation a priority, but it is completely unrealistic to expect that government can consult every stakeholder! Don't wait to be consulted! As I said before, if you guys were on top of environmental scans you may have seen this coming and you could seek out the parties in government who were consulting and put forward your views."

"What about participating through the committee?"

"Possibly an option, if it even goes that far. But don't wait for the committee to be struck. Generally once these things hit the floor of the House it's really too late to do much about it."

After a brief pause, Gabe said quietly, "So we're out of luck then."

"Not necessarily. Remember government timelines are long for many reasons, and frequently this can work in your favour. You have some options available, but I suggest you start with your local MP and have Earl conduct some serious environmental scan analysis. If you need help I know some public relations specialists who could give you a hand, but first you must determine how real this thing is and be able to frame this issue in a manner that clearly demonstrates advantages to the government as well as to RRTC. Remember the government works for all constituents!"

With that, Gabe ended the discussion and hung up the telephone, then set off to find Earl.

Universal Silicon Inc.

James Heathrow gazed out over the Pacific Ocean from his office on the tenth floor of the Universal Silicon Inc. (USI) complex in Northern British Columbia (B.C.) and reflected on the beauty of the surrounding natural environment. Only three years before his "office environment" was quite different—a skyscraper in downtown Toronto that certainly had a view but nothing like this. A chemical engineer by profession with a Master's degree in business, Heathrow had considerable experience in both innovation and management have worked for three Fortune 500 companies (in Canada, the United States and Japan) in very senior executive positions over the past twenty-five years. Since joining USI as its CEO three years ago Heathrow reflected on how this most recent "rodeo" had required that he use every bit of his experience to manage USI successfully.

Company Background

USI was a relatively new leading-edge manufacturer of silicone chips used in personal computers, automobiles, and commercial aircraft. It was established initially as a private corporation with venture funding from two angel investors who recognized the incredible potential value of the intellectual property rights contained in both the manufacturing process and unique materials. Within two years USI "went public" meaning that it transformed from a private corporation to a public corporation selling its shares to the public on the TSX. That was five years ago—today USI is a highly successful corporation providing its shareholders with a return on investment that greatly exceeds the industry standard, with financial statements that are the envy of its competitors. USI is primarily an export business and services, markets the United States, the United Kingdom, China, and Japan where offices are maintained.

At its inception USI started literally in a garage in Mississauga with two computer engineers developing a prototype of a "smart chip." Venture capitalists backed the engineers to form "Smart Chip Inc." that relocated to its current site in Northern B.C. Attracted by the abundant supply of very high quality fresh water from the mountain streams and underground water table (fresh water is essential for silicon chip manufacturing) Smart Chip found the perfect "building"—a government-owned but abandoned former railway station with operational railroad tracks. The company timing was perfect. The federal government, interested in stimulating economic activity in the region, was willing to entertain a public–private partnership through which the government would "sell" the location to the company for a very good price and provide the financing for the purchase at a very low interest rate. In return, the company would develop the chip manufacturing site. During the time that the current complex was being built, Smart Chip Inc. became Universal Silicone Incorporated and went public. The facility was completed within the third year of operations *and* the government was completely paid back. Now everything was owned by USI. Of course the "fairy tale" maturity of USI was not without its challenges and even now the challenges continue.

Growing Pains

Heathrow vividly recalled arriving at USI three years ago. It was only the second year of operations as a publicly traded company and this of course greatly increased the reporting complexities. Fortunately the company had excellent lawyers and accountants so it was able to master the intricacies of "public ownership" in terms of financial reporting but there were other serious "challenges." Notwithstanding the support received from the government in the public–private partnership arrangement Heathrow felt that the actual costs went a bit beyond interest to include what he referred to as the *frustration factor*. Countless meetings were held with government officials to discuss progress. In meeting the environmental laws associated with "water" what seemed a perfectly logical way to Heathrow in meeting the stringent demands was a complete nonstarter with the government. What they proposed was ridiculous in the view of USI. It sometimes appeared as though neither side shared any common ground with the other and the relationship was frequently adversarial!

During this time, Heathrow reflected on attempting to get the Cabinet involved to move the development of the project forward. What difference did it make that Europe was having a financial crisis! USI was bringing jobs to B.C. All that was required was a simple change to the interpretation of a regulation, but no one in government seemed to be interested. What USI proposed would have been great for USI and its key stakeholders and this was clearly articulated in the 300-page report commissioned by the company with a leading consultancy firm.

Then of course there was the backlash created by "interest groups" in Northern B.C. who claimed that this company was completely socially irresponsible and unethical since its activities would deplete all underground freshwater within two years and that the effluent (the by-product or waste resulting from the manufacturing process) would cause severe air pollution through the incineration process leading to grave consequences for people and animals living near the facility. They mounted an online campaign that resulted in participation and commentaries of so-called stakeholders from as far away as Hawaii! This mess didn't settle down until Heathrow met with representatives of these interest groups, shared his data with them, and promised to work with them—even agreeing to have USI contribute to their foundation to further their work on environmental protection in B.C.

What amazed Heathrow on reflection was how the competition seized every moment to publicly, through the Internet mostly, make a "big deal" out of how USI was attempting to manipulate the government and "buy off" civic activists—none of which was true, however it did provoke some questions from both USI suppliers and its customers.

Hiring staff was a bit challenging in those early days as well. Recruiting top graduates from top universities to "come North" (actually, considerably North!) was not an easy undertaking as the "great outdoors" was not always perceived as an advantage. It was not until USI invested in parks and recreational facilities, subsidized upscale housing within walking distance of the facility, and funded an entire research program at the local university that things began to change. Today USI is the place to work and the company has no problem attracting talent from around the world.

But Heathrow's fondest memory was setting up the foreign offices which he did in his first eighteen months as CEO. He vividly recalled what a dismal failure the individual remuneration "bonus" was in China, how risk averse USI's Japanese manager was in Tokyo, and how the previous female Japanese manager in the Tokyo office had had very little success meeting her targets, despite having graduated from a top Canadian university and working fifteen-hour days. He also recalled the dismal failure of his British manager he transferred to China; he could never manage to deliver anything on time in part because, according to him, his Chinese subordinates would always assure him that things were on target when they rarely were. He was always amazed on how the concept of "urgent" and "now" differed between the countries in which USI had offices.

The Challenges of Maturity

For the most part the growing pains had passed, but the challenges persisted and are growing in complexity. Recently the government has launched a consultation on proposed changes to the tax regulations that would make research and development costs in any manufacturing process that did not directly result in improvements in the environment ineligible for deductions against income. The idea was to force companies to ensure that the environment was always taken into account—if your manufacturing process was improved but the effect of this process on the environment could not be demonstrated as improved as a result of the process, then all the research and development invested in improving the process could not be written off as an expense. This was potentially disastrous for USI since it could mean that unless USI could reduce the toxicity level of its incineration process (already well below industry average) the company would not be able to "write off" the costs of its research and development activities. The result would be the company would pay considerably more taxes resulting in less return on investments to shareholders. Heathrow pondered what to do about this.

Another issue confronting USI had to do with corporate social responsibility. For Heathrow, corporate social responsibility, or CSR, was the manner in which a corporation achieves a balance among its economic, social, and environmental responsibilities in its operations so as to address shareholder and other stakeholder expectations. This was complicated. He knew from experience, it was impossible to satisfy every stakeholder and their "stakes." On the other hand, key stakeholders needed to be satisfied to the extent possible. The challenge he was having was the more successful USI became, the more stakeholders came forward, frequently with only vague notions of what their "stake" in the company was. USI was already heavily involved in corporate giving, volunteerism, sponsorship, and philanthropy, and Heathrow believed the investments made through these initiatives resulted in longer-term gains to USI. He was also aware that such investments were made at the expense of the shareholders.

His contemplations were interrupted by his intercom. The Chairman of USI's board of directors was on the telephone.

Questions

1. What is a public–private partnership? What type of public–private partnership did USI have with the government?

2. While involved with the government in the public–private partnership, Heathrow refers to the "frustration factor." What might explain this in the context of the USI-government relations?

3. What errors in dealing with the government have been demonstrated by USI?

4. Which roles of civil society were demonstrated by the "interest groups"?

Friends of Canada's Freshwaters

Jim Baxter could hardly believe what he was reading in the Mountain River Times—a small community-based newspaper produced for the community of Fast River, Alberta. Today's headline: "Council to Support Rafting of Caustic Chemicals." The writer, Calvin O'Hara was praising early indications that the Fast River Municipal Council would allow the Blue Chip Manufacturing Company (BCMC) to transport its chemical wastes in a newly developed "environment-friendly" raft on Fast River to a depot located at the river basin where it would be loaded on to a railway car for transport to an incinerator 150 miles away. In return, BCMC would pay an "environmental tax" to the community of Fast River, citing savings over the standard practice of trucking the wastes to the depot as the reason for its giving back to the community.

In a previous life, Baxter had worked in the silicon chip manufacturing industry and knew only too well the caustic nature of some of the by-products of some of the manufacturing processes. In his current role as researcher for the Friends of Canada's Freshwaters (FCF), a grass-roots organization dedicated to the protection of Canadian freshwater from pollution caused by industry, he was appalled that this proposed practice of BCMC could be supported by any elected officials.

Baxter's telephone calls to BCMC went unanswered and his emails were ignored. He was informed by the Mountain River Times that O'Hara was actually a retired resident of Fast River, currently residing in Florida, who, from time to time wrote articles on matters he thought would be of interest. The Editor of the Mountain River Times however indicated that he would certainly be open to publishing opposing viewpoints, in the interest of solid journalism.

In response, Baxter prepared an "open letter to the people of Fast River" that was published the following week. In his letter he encouraged the people of Fast River to not support this BCMC proposal without a detailed environmental assessment and to ensure the council even had the authority to approve such a proposal. His letter also reported on some research he had undertaken regarding the largely unproven safety record of the "high-tech raft" that was being proposed as the conduit, and outlined the potential damage that could be caused by an accident on the river if one of these rafts upset and the containers failed. He also invited public opinion to the FCF website where his open letter was also posted along with supporting references for every contention he advanced as to why this proposal of BCMC was not optimal. As a final touch, he emailed his network of supporters of FCF, including many international supporters as well as other civil society organizations with either a direct or peripheral interest in the work of FCF.

Within twenty-four hours, the FCF website recorded 24,000 hits and Baxter received over 200 emails from stakeholders, including the provincial government, the federal government, the manufacturer of the raft, the container design engineer, and the national media. The Fast River council was inundated with requests for additional information and received over 400 emails, many from its citizens, expressing nonsupport for the BCMC initiative. A community group from South Africa wrote the council to caution Fast River on their dealings with BCMC indicating that their small community, also located on a river, was where BCMC did their "proof of concept testing" which resulted in two spills before they "got it right" and wiped out the marine ecosystem in the river basin—their letter posted on the FCF website and in the Mountain River Times. All levels of government were being criticized for their handling of the situation.

Two weeks later the Fast River Council unanimously voted against the BCMC proposal and had retained an independent environmental assessment company to assess the environmental practices of BCMC in its current operations. The provincial and federal governments were reported to be watching the situation very carefully.

Robert Hinton's Janitorial Cleaning Service

Robert Hinton[24] owned and operated a janitorial cleaning service in Windsor and had a number of contracts to clean office buildings. At any point in time he needed forty cleaners and he was usually a few short. Not only was he constantly recruiting, he frequently needed to employ illegal immigrants to get the work done. While he paid

---

[24] Case written by Dr. David H J Delcorde, the Telfer School of Management, University of Ottawa, 2010. This case is fictitious. Any resemblance to persons or organizations is purely coincidental.

everyone what he thought was a fair wage, his "undocumented" employees were paid 20 percent less since, he reasoned, they were not paying taxes to the government.

His "staff" reflected an interesting cultural mix and included among the legal workers and the "undocumented" workers, people from China, Norway, and Mexico. He was always amazed how some cultures easily followed instructions and never questioned authority, while others seemed to feel that no one should be in charge because everyone was equal. As well, changing routes or building assignments weekly was intended to provide workers with a bit of variety, but some of these workers could barely tolerate these changes. Some of his workers were very patient and thorough in their work while for some others "reasonably clean" was "clean enough."

Hinton always considered himself as ethical and socially responsible who ran an ethical and socially responsible company. For Hinton, his corporation owed a duty to society as it was, in his view, a social institution with social responsibilities. He even used his own "company developed" garbage bags that were easier on the environment, and moreover, although they cost his clients a little more, for each garbage bag used, he contributed ten cents to "Friends of Windsor's Landfills," a grassroots environmental organization. Dubbed the "Hinton Garbage Bag" these bags were developed through a partnership with Southeastern University's Faculty of Engineering for which Hinton provided a $50,000 research grant that the provincial government matched. Recently many waste-management companies were using these "environmentally friendly" garbage bags.

In early 2019, Robert received a letter from the federal government indicating that his branded garbage bags could no longer be used because the company producing the bags refused to disclose its raw materials' input list, arguing it was patented and private intellectual property. This was a huge problem for Robert because he had just taken delivery of 10,000 bags—enough inventory to hold him through this year of operations. Robert turned to Clem "The Spindoctor" Lewis, an old friend and an experienced lobbyist. Robert hired him, put him on the company payroll for a couple of months, and instructed him to do whatever he had to do—to which Clem decided, given the nature of the issues, to first approach *"the idiot bureaucrat who signed the letter."*

While Clem was developing his strategy, Robert was surfing the web one evening and discovered a Facebook group started by a member of Friends of Windsor's Landfills, expressing the opinion that forcing Robert's company to stop using the branded garbage bags was the very same as the government condoning "environmental irresponsibility." The Facebook membership was approaching 5,000! Moreover, from following the message trails it became apparent that what was driving this issue was a piece of federal government legislation, sponsored by the federal Minister of the Environment, to reduce the use of "Carbon Twenty Nine," a compound that accelerated decay of hydrocarbons that, although assisting in speeding up the decaying process of garbage and reducing the volume of garbage in landfills, had also been found to cause cancer in fish, in early but as yet unproven laboratory research conducted by the Taiwanese scientists. Carbon Twenty Nine was a key component in the "Hinton" garbage bags.

Robert shook his head thoughtfully, amazed at how complicated things had become in running a simple "no-tech" building cleaning company!

Required

Respond to each of the following questions:

1. Robert's given a reason for paying his undocumented workers 20 percent less means that he is an unethical person

_____ T _____ F

2. Suppose that Robert felt his decision to pay his undocumented workers less than his "documented, legal" workers was morally correct, did not disrespect the dignity of others and he was comfortable if the decision to pay undocumented workers less became known as the "Robert Hinton Decision." This would pass:

   a. The Justice Test

   b. The Deontological Test

   c. The Test of Consequentialism

   d. The Ethics Test of Certainty

3. Clem Lewis would be considered:

   a. A consultant lobbyist

   b. An in-house lobbyist (corporations)

   c. An in-house lobbyist (organizations)

   d. A contracted lobbyist

4. Hinton's view of his company having social responsibilities would support which one of the following categories of social responsibility?

   a. Amoral view

   b. Personal view

   c. Social view

   d. Moral view

5. Hinton's contribution to "Friends of Windsor's Landfills" best represents:

   a. Strategic giving

   b. Social Enterprise

   c. Social venture philanthropy

   d. Cause-related marketing

Lobbying

6. Clem's decision to approach the bureaucrat implies that so far as Robert's company is concerned, this is a strategic issue

_____ T _____ F

7. The style of lobbying planned by Clem is:

   a. Direct

   b. Indirect

   c. Advocacy

   d. Think Tank

8. Which one of the following fundamental errors business makes in dealing with government has been made by Clem?

   a. Dealing only with politicians

   b. Providing time-like reports to politicians

   c. Wading in on an issue too late

   d. Reacting to government on an issue-by-issue basis

Cultural Considerations (Hofstede's Cultural Dimensions)

9. Robert Hinton's staff members have a range of cultural back-grounds—Canadian, Mexican, Chinese, and Norwegian. Those cultures who accept the uneven distribution of power would be described by Hofstede as having greater _____ _____and would most likely be found in his workers who come from _____.

10. His workers who would demonstrate the greatest amount of mod-esty and caring would likely come from _____. These workers would likely display a level of _____ _____ similar to Canadian workers.

11. The workers most likely having the greatest difficulty adjusting to unpredictable and constantly changing routes would be those from _____ who would likely also demonstrate the lowest level of _____ from among the Chinese, Norwegians, Mexicans, and Canadians.

12. Hinton's cleaning staff most likely to work best as a team and be more concerned with how their cleaning "team" is perceived would most likely be workers from China because, relative to the Canadians, Mexicans, and Norwegians it is the most _____ culture.

Influence

13. The Facebook group demonstrates how civil society can influence business through publishing campaigns

_____ T _____ F

14. If the federal Minister of the Environment is successful in passing the referenced legislation it would be illegal to use the plastic bags developed by Robert Hinton. The imposition of this law represents a form of government _____ regulation.

15. Suppose the federal Minister of the Environment is successful in passing the federal legislation. If the government decided to "buy back" all of the garbage bags in the inventories of all companies who were now using them, this would represent a form of government Subsidy, which is considered to be a form of _____ government influence.

16. If Clem decided to mobilize the Facebook group and collectively take a public stand against the Minister of the Environment's pending legislation without actually selling a product, but rather the idea that these bags are safe for the environment and people, this would represent a form of lobbying referred to as

_____ _____ .

17. Although the federal Minister of the Environment is tabling legislation that would indirectly eliminate the use of Hinton's garbage bags, the provincial government originally provide a research grant to Southeastern University for their development. This information should *not* be used by Clem in dealing with the federal bureaucrat referred to above because the federal government obviously knows what the provincial government is doing.

_____ T _____ F

Index